RUPERT BROOKE
IN CANADA

RUPERT BROOKE
IN CANADA

EDITED BY
SANDRA MARTIN
AND ROGER HALL

PMA BOOKS

Canadian Cataloguing in Publication Data

Brooke, Rupert, 1887-1915.
  Rupert Brooke in Canada

Some articles originally published in the
Westminster gazette.

ISBN 0-88778-184-5

1. Canada – Description and travel – 1900-1950.*
2. Brooke, Rupert, 1887 – 1915. I. Martin, Sandra,
1947-   II. Hall, Roger, 1945-   III. Title.

FC74.B88   917.1'04'61   C78-001518-5
F1015.B88

© 1978 Sandra Martin and Roger Hall

Design: Michael Solomon

ALL RIGHTS RESERVED

Peter Martin Associates Limited
280 Bloor Street West, Toronto, Canada M5S 1W1

CONTENTS

PREFACE

Rupert Brooke published his travel pieces on Canada and the United States in the English weekly *Westminster Gazette* in 1913-1914. After his death they were gathered by his literary executor and friend Edward Marsh and, with some more essays plus a preface by Henry James, appeared as *Letters from America* in 1916. As such they have, over the years, sparked considerable interest, but the volume is now a comparative rarity. *Rupert Brooke in Canada* reprints Brooke's original travel articles concerning Canada along with selected passages from his Canadian correspondence and contemporary photographs of Brooke and the Canada through which he journeyed. Much of the material in this book has never been published before. There is also a substantial introduction and afterword recording Brooke's short life, and explaining his association with Canada.

Many people in both Canada and England have helped in the book's production. We are particularly grateful to Sir Geoffrey Keynes, Brooke's close friend and now the senior trustee of his estate, for granting us access to the Brooke Archive at King's College, Cambridge and permitting us to use formerly unpublished materials. Also at King's thanks go to Peter Croft, the Librarian, and Marion Stewart, Modern Literary Archivist. Miss Cathleen Nesbitt continues in the

British theatre still and we are most grateful for her reminiscences.

The Canadian list is longer. Special thanks go to Gordon Dodds at the Public Archives of Canada, Richard Landon of the Thomas Fisher Library at the University of Toronto, John Gishler and Les Fowlie at the Calgary Public Library, and Albert Bowron of Toronto. Alfred and Louise Hall, Glynis Barnes, Dorothy Sedgwick, and Hunter Bishop, the Archivist of the Arts and Letters Club of Toronto, have also been most helpful. David Cobb read the manuscript and we are grateful for his suggestions. Special thanks to the Ontario Arts Council for their support.

RUPERT BROOKE
IN CANADA

INTRODUCTION

O N 22 May, 1913, a disconsolate little beggar named William waved and cried from the dock as the *S.S. Cedric*, bound for New York, pulled out of Liverpool Harbour. On board, a tall young man with limpid blue eyes returned the salute. Then, flicking his reddish-gold hair back from his brow with a careless and automatic gesture he turned from the rail and went to the purser's office to check the post. A few minutes later, clutching a letter from his sweetheart, he retired to his cabin.

It was an ordinary leave-taking, one of countless such melodramas enacted every week, except that it was a sham. Young William had been paid sixpence for his tears because his handsome patron, Rupert Chawner Brooke—poet, fellow of King's College, Cambridge, and the newly-appointed correspondent of the *Westmister Gazette*—wanted a send-off no matter how paltry or artificial. Brooke was on assignment (expenses plus four guineas an article) to write travel pieces about the United States and Canada.

This book is about Brooke's time in Canada, the journalism he wrote, the letters he sent back home, the people he met, and the country he travelled through. Rupert Brooke was twenty-five when he came to North America. Two years later he would be famous and dead, the national symbol of a generation martyred for a patriotic ideal—an ideal that perished in the trenches of northern France and Belgium.

For most people the name Rupert Brooke is dimly familiar, a figure dredged up from that lumpen galaxy that includes silent screen stars, French explorers, and Canadian Prime Ministers. A few nod in recognition at his lines:

> If I should die, think only this of me
>   That there's some corner of a foreign field
> That is forever England. . . .

Fewer still know that he ever set foot on this continent or that he wrote about it in prose that is candid, humorous, and perceptive.

Most of the writing about Canada in the first years of this century was propaganda, advertising gauged to entice settlers and investors to the new land. Brooke's observations were different. He wrote from a poet's perspective, not from the self-interest of a businessman or immigration agent; he commented on the country's cultural life as well as its balance of payments. For him cities were not merely boundaries, buildings, and statistics, nor the countryside simply so many square miles to be cultivated, stripped, or mined.

At first he didn't like the place much. What he looked for and could not find in Canada was a "soul". By this he meant a cultural identity, a unifying emotional principle that could never be found in statute books and Acts of Parliament. The country was, of course, young; it had neither "ghosts" nor the overlay of generations to soften the contours of the landscape and give it presence. He recognized immediately the alienation between French and English and he prophesied (wrongly) that after Laurier no French Canadian would ever again be Prime Minister.

All this is not to suggest that Brooke was entirely negative about Canada. He came, a talented and arrogant young man, to observe the country and be toughened by it. His knowledge and understanding grew as he moved further west and his observations and insights sharpened correspondingly. Whether hiking through the woods, canoeing on remote lakes, or arguing poetry and politics at the Arts and Letters Club in Toronto, Brooke encountered Canada as it was in that palpable hush before the First World War destroyed everything, forever. And what he saw, he recorded with a skill and insight that makes the articles as fresh today as when they were first published sixty-five years ago.

Rupert Brooke was born on 3 August 1887 in Rugby in the English Midlands, the second of three sons of William Parker Brooke and his wife Ruth Mary Cotterill. His school-teacher father, "Tooler" to his students, soon became Master of School Field, one of the constituent houses of the famous public school that Dr. Thomas Arnold had moulded and on which Thomas Hughes later based *Tom Brown's Schooldays*. Rupert's mother, "Ma Tooler", was iron-willed and implacable, an intelligent, humourless Victorian.

Brooke went to a local preparatory school, Hillbrow, where he played cricket well, voraciously consumed library books, toyed with an alternative magazine to the Rugby School paper, excelled in French, Latin, and English, and suffered frequently from pink-eye and sore throat; he was nicknamed Oyster.

At Hillbrow Rupert met Lytton Strachey's younger brother James, the earliest of his life-long friends and the first in an ever-widening circle that would eventually form a Rupert Brooke cult. "At least the markings of glamour were already there," James Strachey recalled decades later about his schoolboy friend.

Rupert entered Rugby School in September 1901, a new boy at his father's house, School Field. It was an odd arrangement being sent to boarding school in your own home, but aside from one prank (Mrs. Brooke opened the dumbwaiter one lunchtime to discover Rupert, cross-legged on the shelf with a note pinned on his chest, "Mother, behold thy son"), Rupert's schoolmates ignored his filial connection to the "Tooler".

It was at Rugby that Rupert began writing serious poetry. In 1904 he came second in the annual poetry competition with "The Pyramids" and a year later won a collection of the works of Browning and Rossetti for "The Bastille". He was greatly influenced by St. John Lucas, an Old Rugbeian and now a "decadent" poet and the editor of *The Oxford Book of French Verse*. Rupert began studying the works of Baudelaire and the then popular English poet Ernest Dowson. He was also reading Hilaire Belloc from whom he contracted—not unusual for one of his time and class—a dose of anti-semitism. As well, he began entering, frequently with success, the weekly literary competitions in the *Westminster Gazette*, a link that later would pay his way to America.

At school his closest friends were Hugh Russell-Smith and Geoffrey Keynes, the younger brother of the economist John Maynard Keynes. It was through the younger members of the Strachey and Keynes families that Rupert was later introduced to Bloomsbury, the literary and artistic mafia that dominated British intellectual life in the first decades of this century.

Sir Geoffrey Keynes, now in his nineties, is Rupert's only surviving childhood friend. As senior trustee he controls the Brooke Archive at King's College, Cambridge, stalwartly protecting after death the friend he loved and admired in life. No true psychological portrait of Rupert Brooke will be possible until Keynes's vigilance is relaxed and all the letters and papers are opened. In the meantime, researchers must rely heavily on the official biography written by former Brooke trustee, the late Christopher Hassall.

The world has changed since Rupert and Geoffrey were classmates at Rugby. The Victorian Gothic buildings with their navy and yellow Italianate designs etched in the red brick walls still encircle the close. And the monstrous chapel replete with fairytale gargoyles (designed by Sir Herbert Butterfield in 1872) must still strike fear in the souls of errant schoolboys. Otherwise, much is different. Nowadays, students slouch across the close on weekends in tattered jeans and live in bedrooms plastered with pin-ups and lurid posters. In Rupert's day, "fagging"—that barbaric custom whereby seniors enslaved juniors—was in full flower and not only was there a strict dress code, but rigidly imposed modes of behaviour.

In his last term at Rugby Rupert was ranked among the first XI, a status that allowed him to add a blue ribbon to the plain white straw hat that tradition demanded he wore cocked at an angle. As a senior he could walk with both hands in his pockets and all his books tucked under one arm. He was inviolate, head of his house and a school swell, and he loved it. At the end of term he wrote to Geoffrey Keynes, "This school-life, with its pathetic transience and immense vitality, calls to me with a charm all the more insistent that I am soon to lose it." A few weeks later he graduated, having won both the King's Medal for Prose for his essay on England's debt to William III, and a scholarship to King's College, Cambridge. He was eighteen.

The alienating asceticism of Cambridge was a shock after the adulation of Rugby. From his room in "A" staircase at King's, Rupert wrote home, "I try not to notice the wallpaper." About the same time he wrote to his cousin Erica Cotterill, "I find this place absolutely devoid of interest and amusement. I like nobody. They all seem dull, middle-aged, and ugly." Partly he was suffering from a surfeit of "decadence", that bored and boring pose he had borrowed from St. John Lucas. But mainly Rupert was homesick. He had friends at Cambridge, particularly Geoffrey Keynes at Pembroke and James Strachey at Trinity, but it was Rupert's first time living away from home and as much as he chafed under his mother's dominating hand, he missed her.

Within the first weeks of his arrival Rupert met Hugh Dalton who had just come up from Eton, Justin Brooke (no relation) of Emmanuel College, and Edward Marsh, a Trinity graduate and private secretary to Winston Churchill. Each would influence him profoundly and introduce him to a circle of friends that in the end would make Rupert as celebrated a figure in London society and in King's Parade as ever he had been on the close at Rugby.

Eddie Marsh gradually replaced St. John Lucas as Rupert's literary mentor and agent. Their friendship began slowly, but by 1910 Brooke was regularly sending work to Marsh for criticism, and more often, approval. At his flat in Gray's Inn,

London, Marsh introduced Brooke to an amusing and talented assortment of poets, politicians, and actresses. And when Rupert was in America, Eddie proved a valuable and friendly correspondent, full of news, advice, and encouragement.

With Justin Brooke Rupert founded the Marlowe Dramatic Society, dedicated to performing Elizabethan plays in verse not prose. Although Rupert was stiff and self-conscious on stage, he appeared in most of the society's productions and in *Comus* (performed in early summer of 1908 for the Tercentenary of Milton's birth), he not only played one of the principal roles, the Attendant Spirit, but produced the play as well.

With Hugh Dalton he founded the *Carbonari* (the charcoal burners) in honour of the nineteenth-century Italian revolutionary society. Along with some carefully chosen associates they met in one another's rooms to read papers and declaim poetry, but they were far more interested in railing against the stifling puritanism of the Victorian age than effecting any concrete political or social change.

More as a lark than from any sense of commitment Rupert had helped his mother propel the local Liberal candidate into power in the general election of January 1906. Back at Cambridge under the influence of Hugh Dalton, Rupert became increasingly interested in serious politics and particularly Fabianism, the British socialist movement that had helped to found the Labour Party in 1900.

The Fabian Society, founded in 1884, was perfectly calculated to attract young liberals like Rupert. It was a middle-class intellectual pressure-group convinced that socialism was best brought about not by the violence inherent in Marxist dogma, but by gradual constitutional reforms. Its most famous adherents were people like Sidney and Beatrice Webb, George Bernard Shaw, and H. G. Wells. The Cambridge University Fabian Society was founded in 1906. Among its early advocates were Margery Olivier, the daughter of founding member Sydney Olivier, and Katharine "Ka"

Cox, a freshman at Newnham and next to his mother, probably the most disturbing and important woman in Rupert's short life. At first Rupert was cautious about committing himself to Fabianism and it wasn't until early 1908 that he took the oath (or signed "The Basis"). Once having made that step Brooke committed himself completely. What had started as a schoolboy rebellion against everything Victorian had now coalesced into an all-consuming political passion. His particular focus was the reform of the Poor Laws.

The Poor Laws legislation of 1834 was based on the premise that prosperity was a direct result of industriousness. Therefore, indiscriminate handouts from local governments, whether secular or parish-based, only encouraged idleness and resulted in poverty. Poor people were by definition lazy, indigents who could find relief from hunger and destitution only in the Workhouse, that dank, cheerless institution described so effectively by Charles Dickens in *Oliver Twist*. This system, with slight modification, lasted into the twentieth century.

Brooke and the Fabians wanted government to recognize its responsibilities to the industrial working class by enacting, among other schemes, a social insurance policy. The apogee of Fabian enthusiasm in Poor Law Reform coincided with Brooke's tenure as third president of the Cambridge University Fabian Society (1909-1910) when the local group grew to 105 full members and 142 associates. Brooke led the university delegation to a Fabian conference in London in June 1910 and spent much of the remaining summer stumping the countryside preaching that Poor Law Reform would strengthen the moral fibre of the nation and ensure industrial peace and productivity. In his last address as president to the Cambridge Society, in December 1910, Brooke anticipated, by some thirty years, the British Arts Council when he called for annual government assistance to creative artists.

When David Lloyd-George, Chancellor of the Exchequer in the Asquith government, brought in the National Insurance Act in 1911-12 and with it a measure of health and unemployment insurance for the working classes, much of the impetus for Fabian reform disappeared. Shortly thereafter, Brooke too lost his zeal for Poor Law Reform although he remained intellectually committed to Fabianism.

Besides Fabianism, the *Carbonari*, and the Marlowe Dramatic Society, Rupert had been elected in 1908 to the governing board of the *Cambridge Review*, and to the Cambridge *Conversazione* Society or the "Apostles" as it was more commonly called. Membership in that secret and select society included Lytton and James Strachey, John Maynard Keynes, Bertrand Russell, Leonard Woolf, G. E. Moore, Goldsworthy Lowes Dickenson, and previously, Lord Tennyson, Walter Raleigh, and Arthur Hallam. All this left little time for studying, particularly the Classics which Rupert considered not only dead but deadly. He did miserably in the examinations in May 1908, and managed only a poor second when he wrote the Tripos the following year.

By the autumn of 1909 Rupert had decided to abandon the Classics for English Literature and to recoup his academic fortunes by submitting an essay on the English dramatist John Webster for the Oldham Shakespeare scholarship. More important, he determined to live out of college, at "The Orchard", a cottage in Grantchester, a village about three miles from the university. Far from isolating him, The Orchard became a conveniently comfortable place for his friends to gather. "We used to loll in armchairs and talk wearily about Art and Suicide and the Sex Problem," the artist Gwen Raverat recalled years later.

Rupert no longer found Cambridge odious. At the beginning of Michaelmas term, 1909, his friend Hugh Dalton asked him whether the latest crop of freshmen made him feel old. "No," came the reply. "Not old. Only tremendous." And indeed he was. In September he had won two contests in the *Westminster Gazette* and had had four poems published in *The English Review*; in October he was included in Hugh Dalton's article, "Those in Authority" in *Granta*; and in December he won the Oldham Prize for his essay on Webster. Marks were but a trifle compared with Rupert's stature as poet, debater, critic, intellectual, socialist, and all-round beauty—"A young Apollo, golden haired," as his friend Frances Darwin (later Cornford) scribbled in a poem that was sticky in its sentimentality and simplistic in its perspective. After his death that epigram became enormously popular and for most people served as a definition of the man.

But even more persistent than the "Young Apollo" legend is the myth that Rupert Brooke was a homosexual. Despite his six-foot height, he had a feminine beauty and a translucent skin that betrayed every blush. Certainly he knew homosexuals, particularly among his Bloomsbury friends, and while at Rugby, Rupert was amused in a disdainful, superior way by a crush another boy suffered for him. Perhaps the greatest boost to the homosexual theory came after his death. When Rupert's great friend and literary executor Edward Marsh published his *Memoir* in 1918, he drew heavily upon Brooke's letters including love notes to the actress Cathleen Nesbitt. Rupert's mother insisted these be labelled "to a friend" and so the public assumed Marsh's reticence protected a homosexual lover.

It is quite probable that James Strachey made passes at Rupert and equally probable that Rupert repelled them. Certainly Rupert had a violent break with Bloomsbury in 1912 and while he eventually effected a cool peace with James he never reconciled with his brother Lytton. The cause of the rupture was Ka Cox, Rupert's old Cambridge friend. She was in love with the Bloomsbury painter Henry Lamb (one of Lytton Strachey's early infatuations) and Rupert, maddened by jealousy, demanded that she give up Lamb and marry him. Ka refused, and in his desperation Rupert blamed Lytton for promoting the "affair" between Ka and Henry Lamb and then all of Bloomsbury for contaminating Ka with their intellectualism and worst of all their feminism. It was, of course, nonsense, but Rupert was not used to being thwarted and for all his protestations he was at heart a Victorian. The dichotomy between his deep-seated Victorianism and his self-proclaimed hedonism resulted finally in a series of breakdowns in 1912.

Unlike his pacifist Bloomsbury friends Brooke was an arch-Imperialist who would march off to war in 1914 as eagerly as all the other bright and beautiful young men. And he abhored feminism—"that denial of sex . . . with its resultant shallowness of woman and degradation of man"—with an irrational passion. He considered Strindberg the foremost of contemporary playwrights because of his anti-feminist stance and consequently dismissed Ibsen, the author of *A Doll's House*, as that "great and dirty playwright". But perhaps Rupert's most classic Victorian attribute was his belief in the double standard. Women he loved were to be idealized, the rest were for trifling.

His first love was Noel, the young sister of his Fabian compatriot Margery Olivier. She was the subject of much of the poetry in *Poems, 1911*, the only book Rupert published before his death. Brooke worshipped Noel with an adolescent fervour, striking absurd poses and concocting ludicrous schemes for chance encounters. But it wasn't until 1910, two years after their meeting at a Fabian dinner, that Rupert declared himself. Yet even while Noel was accepting Rupert's devotions, he was becoming inexorably entangled with Ka Cox. He was torn between the two women and he agonized over the loyalty and commitment he owed each; when Sidgwick & Jackson brought out Rupert's *Poems* the following year he tried to dedicate the book to Noel, but she refused.

In January 1911 Rupert went to Munich to learn German for he had decided to revise his Oldham essay on John Webster in hopes of winning a fellowship at King's. In fact, he sat in cafés writing poetry, being homesick, and paying little heed to the German voices around him. He maintained his copious friendships by post, but his friends were either pairing off or moving into other phases of their lives. He felt very much alone, except for Ka. Ka was everything Rupert's mother was not—soothing, warm, empathetic, and supportive. And after returning to England in May, Rupert spent the rest of the year running from his mother in Rugby to Noel Olivier to Ka. It culminated in December in that wild scene in which he demanded Ka give up Henry Lamb and marry him. Brooke was exhausted emotionally, physically, and spiritually and in January 1912 he had his first breakdown.

For a while he recuperated in Cannes under the watchful eye of the "Ranee" as he now called his mother. (Rupert had only just learned that for years Lytton Strachey had been calling him the Rajah because he had the same name as Sir James Brooke, Rajah of Sarawak; the nickname delighted Rupert and he handed on the female version to his mother.) While the Ranee was feeding him tonics, Rupert was writing desperate and mad letters to Ka pleading for rescue and begging her to join him in Munich where he felt sure she would be able to nurse him back to health. Eventually Ka and Rupert met in Verona, in Italy, and travelled to Munich where they lived together for a few weeks. Kind, generous Ka agreed to be Rupert's lover because she felt sorry for him and she genuinely feared for his sanity. For Rupert the loss of his virginity turned him against Ka and destroyed his love for her. She had been soiled by her association with the Bloomsbury crowd, but now he had definite physical proof of her humanity and that disgusted him.

Ironically, Ka now fell desperately in love with Rupert. Nineteen-twelve was an appalling year with Ka and Rupert loving and fighting and parting only to begin the wretched cycle all over again. In April Brooke learned he had failed to win the fellowship at King's—a not unexpected but still bitter blow. For months he wandered between Berlin and England wavering on the edges of breakdown and suicide one minute and in a manic and creative euphoria the next.

The year was not all horror: sitting in the Café des Westens in May 1912, mooning about Ka, Rupert dashed off "The Sentimental Exile" or, as it is better known, "The Old Vicarage, Grantchester". It's a lively though sentimental piece that recalls the wonders of Grantchester and the other villages around Cambridge. "Stands the Church clock at ten to three?/And is there honey still for tea?" are the most famous lines. (Indeed, after Brooke's death there was a movement to stop the church clock permanently at this hour as a crazy sort of memorial.) He sent the poem off to Cambridge in time to be included in the June issue of *Basileon*, the King's magazine. Later it was published in *Poetry Review* and won him £30 as the best *Review* poem of 1912.

Back in England Rupert allowed his friend Frances Cornford to convince him that recovery lay in hard physical labour and a complete separation from Ka; Mrs. Cornford's notion of a convalescent spa was a fruit farm in California. Although he still suffered relapses, Brooke was on the mend. He was back at The Old Vicarage in Grantchester to which he had moved from The Orchard in January 1911, but he was spending more and more time in London, principally at Eddie Marsh's flat in Gray's Inn. It was a good place for him, away from the isolation of The Old Vicarage where he was revising his Webster dissertation for another try at the King's fellowship, and away from the Cambridge friends who were a constant reminder of Noel and Ka. Rupert was entering a new stage, that of the professional poet.

By day Eddie worked at the Admiralty where Winston Churchill was now First Lord, but by night he worked equally hard as a literary impresario. He knew all the young poets and artists and not only promoted their work but often paid their rent from a private income he referred to as "murder money". Marsh's great-grandfather had been Spencer Perceval, the only British prime minister ever to be assassinated. His family had been granted compensation by parliament and Eddie's share (one-sixth) still arrived annually. It was this "murder money" that Eddie used to buy paintings and poems from the young (and often destitute) artists and writers he admired.

And it was with this "murder money" that he and Brooke proposed to launch the anthology *Georgian Poetry* in September 1912. The name both honoured George V who had ascended the throne two years before and emphasized that the collection was modern poetry for a modern age and not in any way connected with Victorianism. Marsh was to be editor, Harold Monro's Poetry Bookshop would serve as publishing house, and the "murder money" would guarantee any losses. In all, five volumes of *Georgian Poetry* appeared between 1912 and 1922. Among the thirty-six contributors were Walter de la Mare, John Masefield, Siegfried Sassoon, D. H. Lawrence, Robert Graves, and, of course, Rupert Brooke. The anthologies were wildly popular and gave rise to the Georgian movement which encompassed all that was modern and innovative—for a time anyway.

In December 1912 Rupert met the beautiful young actress Cathleen Nesbitt at a party in Eddie's flat. In her autobiography, *A Little Love & Good Company*, Cathleen described the Rupert she knew then:

> Rupert, though I did not know it till long afterwards, was still rather neurotic and depressed after an unhappy love affair. He had been desperately in love with someone else, but who, out of kindness and pity, had consented to live with him for a time. During that time she fell in love with him, but he had grown out of love with her. He thought she was with child by him, and she had a miscarriage for which he bitterly blamed himself. He was still suffering from a guilt complex.

The woman was undoubtedly Ka, but since the Cox letters have been sealed by the Brooke trustees, one can't confirm the information about the aborted pregnancy. Certainly, it makes sense of many of the cryptic comments about "love", "murder", and "children" that appear both in Sir Geoffrey Keynes's edition of *The Letters of Rupert Brooke* and in Christopher Hassall's official biography, and it explains Rupert's emotional collapse. Free love, abortion on demand, and unmarried mothers were subjects not even to be discussed in polite society, let alone condoned. It was a time when, as Rupert, ironically, once wrote to Ka, "we don't copulate without marriage".

Rupert was not going to risk a repeat of the Ka affair with Cathleen. "When we spent the night at a country inn," she explained in her autobiography, "we had separate rooms. He would come in and sit on the edge of my bed and talk almost till dawn, but strange as it may seem to anyone of this generation we never actually became lovers in the sense that he seduced me, as the contemporary phrase would have it."

No, Cathleen was to be worshipped, preserved, and above all kept pure—even if he weren't around to stand guard.

He wrote to her from Rugby in May 1913, "I hate your going anywhere or doing anything while I'm away. Will you kindly pass the next nine months in a state of suspended animation?" From America he sent long loving letters, but good Victorian that he was, he never mentioned (as he did in letters to Eddie) flirting with a girl named Louise in New York State, or the liaison he had with the widow Marchesa Capponi in Lake Louise, or the long affair in Tahiti with the native woman Taatamata.

By 1913 there was little reason for Rupert to leave England. Ka was no more than a familiar dull ache, he was in love with Cathleen, and in March he finally won his fellowship at King's. Still he had promised Frances Cornford to go away and he was determined to keep his word. Then in May, Naomi Royde-Smith, the literary editor of the *Westminster Gazette*, provided both the spur and the money for Rupert's tour. Knowing Brooke was willing to travel, she showed a prose piece he had written the year before to her editor, J. A. Spender, and proposed that Brooke be hired to write travel pieces about America. Spender agreed. And so it was settled.

I

RUPERT boarded the Montreal Express in New York on 29 June 1913 for the overnight train journey to Montreal. He had been in "Noo York" as he called it, with the exception of a jaunt in the country and an excursion to Boston, for almost a month. Overall he didn't like America much, and he liked New York a good deal less. He wrote to Cathleen Nesbitt, "This is *not* a land for a civilized man. There are three things worth some praise; the architecture, the children's clothes, and the jokes. All else is flatulence and despair and a living Death." But he had made some friends, and as he grew more comfortable in their society he became more appreciative of the country—"some country" as he was told continually.

Brooke had a grudging admiration for crass New York where "Business has developed insensibly into a Religion". He admired the skyscrapers and thought Fifth Avenue "the handsomest street imaginable ... what the streets of German Cities try to be". But Boston with its "curiously English" quality and "delicious Ancient Toryism" was more to his taste:

It sits in comfortable middle-age, on the ruins of its glory. But it is not buried beneath them. It used to lead America in Literature, Thought, Art, everything. The years have passed. It is remarkable how nearly now Boston is to New York what Munich is to Berlin. ... If Berlin and New York are more 'live,'

Boston and Munich are more themselves, less feverishly imitations of Paris.

He liked Harvard (across the river at Cambridge), although Cambridge, Mass. wasn't the Cambridge he knew, and he busied himself with the inevitable comparisons. He was there for the festivities and rituals of commencement week which included his first baseball game—"merely glorified rounders" —and a marchpast of alumni ranked by year (with a noticeable gap marking the American Civil War). He concluded that "American universities keep putting up the most wonderful and expensive buildings. But they do not pay their teachers well." Still he was taken by a certain Harvard "spirit, a way of looking at things, austerely refined, gently moral, kindly". What stuck with him when he crossed the border, as he later wrote to his friend Edward Marsh, was American "hospitality"—a quality, he found, quite absent in Canada:

> Lord, Lord—I've not really given the Canadians much chance yet. But my impression is that they have all the faults of the Americans, and not their one lovely and redeeming virtue, 'hospitality'. That 'hospitality' is often sneered at in the Americans; but it merely means that with the nice ones, you can be at once on happy and intimate terms. Oh dear, the tears quite literally well up when I think of a group of young Harvard people I tumbled into.... they were connected with the theatrical movement there, and they had the charm and freshness and capacity for instantly creating a relation of happy and warm friendliness.... But these people here.... However I fancy the West may be better....

Brooke disliked Montreal, although Canada to him after the United States was a "homecoming", and he recognized "in the untidiness of those grimy houses, the smoky disorder of the backyards", something "that ran a thrill of nostalgia" through him. It was "the English way of doing things" but "with a difference that I could not define till later". That difference, of course, was Canada's French fact—recently given force and voice by Sir Wilfrid Laurier, and more recently still by the strident nationalist champion Henri Bourassa, especially through his newspaper Le Devoir.

Brooke never achieved much understanding of French Canada. In the cities he discovered only the British or more precisely the Scottish elements—the banks and great stone houses in Montreal and the Citadel, the baronial Château Frontenac, the Plains of Abraham, and stately Dufferin Terrace in Quebec City. It wasn't until he reached the settled countryside of the St. Lawrence and later the gloomy shores of the Saguenay that he was at all moved. The Saguenay stirred him deeply, its steep, craggy shores excited his poet's sensibility like no North American city had. Brooke had not intended to go up to Quebec or the Saguenay at all, but the trip, taken on a whim, marked for him a real departure, and a shift to a state of contentment that became obvious in his writings.

Until he reached the St. Lawrence and the Saguenay his work was a record, nothing more—occasionally something less —of skyscrapers, trains, hucksters, nice and nasty people, and foreign places. The Canadian rivers reminded him that North America—significantly, that Canada—was something else: it was nature.

Brooke came to Canada with two letters of introduction— one to Sir Wilfrid Laurier, and the other (given to him by John Masefield) to the Canadian poet Duncan Campbell Scott. He found both in Ottawa, and, in fact, spent more than a week there, much of it at Scott's spacious house on Lisgar Street with its attractive garden. They talked about poets and the literary life, but Brooke also bombarded his Canadian host with questions about the country, and particularly about Indians. For many years Scott had been Superintendent of Indian Education, and had just been made Deputy Superintendent General of Indian Affairs. Brooke was fascinated, but somewhat saddened by Scott's solitary life. He wrote to fellow Georgian Wilfred Gibson, whose books he had found on Scott's shelves:

> The only poet in Canada was very nice to me in Ottawa— Duncan Campbell Scott, aetat. 50, married, an authority on Indians. Poor devil, he's so lonely and dried there: no one to talk to. They had a child—daughter—who died in 1908 or so.

And it knocked them out. She, a violinist, never played since: he hasn't written, till the last few months. Their house was queerly desolate. It rather went to my heart. Canada's a *bloody* place for a sensitive—in a way 2nd rate—real, slight poet like that to live all his life. Nobody cares if he writes or doesn't. He took me out to a Club in the country near, and we drank whisky and soda, and he said 'Well, here's to your youth!' and drank its health, and I nearly burst into tears. He's a very nice chap (especially away from his wife, who's nice enough): and he's *thirsty* to talk literature; and he's very keen on all our work. He saw a little of the 1890-1905 men . . . and he finds us *far* better! So he's obviously to be encouraged.

Poetry gave way to politics when Brooke had lunch with Sir Wilfrid Laurier. In 1913 Laurier was Leader of the Opposition, and perhaps the best-known Imperial statesman outside of England. He was in his early seventies, affable and agreeable, and Brooke was charmed by him. "Laurier was a nice old man," he told his mother, "a bit of a politician; playing the party game, but not so much as the others." The party game which interested Brooke most was the naval question, the arms race that occupied Britain and the Empire during the years leading to the First World War.

Imperial Britain was anxious to have its Empire contribute to the manufacture of battleships (Dreadnoughts) for the Royal Navy: the rapid rate of German production of capital ships in 1909 had caused a crisis and Canada was felt to be dragging its feet. Laurier's policy characterized the balancing act between French and English Canada that marked his whole career. Canada, he had long argued, would *not* simply make contributions to the Royal Navy. To do so would be against both the spirit and substance of Canadian self-government. The best plan, he announced in 1910, would be to create a Canadian navy that in times of war could become part of the Imperial fleet. Laurier's compromise, his Liberals thought, would satisfy most Canadians: autonomy, but within the Empire.

Robert Borden's Conservatives railed against "Laurier's tin-pot navy" and demanded that Canada should immediately supply Britain with the cost of two capital ships. English

Canada was swayed by thoughts of the duties and glories of the Empire, and convinced that Laurier had gone too far. French Canada was equally certain that he had not gone far enough. Henri Bourassa, the chief spokesman for French-Canadian opposition, saw Laurier's compromise as kowtowing to the Imperial masters of London. In the election of 1911 the vote was clearly split, a split further felt because the Liberals had resurrected the notion of trade reciprocity with the United States. By the time of Brooke's visit in 1913 the country was still badly divided. The new Prime Minister, Robert Borden, had secured an appropriation of $35 million for Imperial shipbuilding, but the Liberals had managed to stop the bill in the Senate. All was suspended in the summer of 1914 when war broke out and Canada found itself automatically involved.

Brooke was both an English patriot and a fervent Imperialist. His Englishness provided at first the main measure of everything he saw abroad, and his Imperial attitudes directly reflected the opinions of his new London circle of friends, closest of whom was Edward Marsh, private secretary to Winston Churchill, First Lord of the Admiralty. From Toronto Brooke wrote Marsh that "the most unpopular person in Canada was Winston . . . they *do* hate him". The reason was simple: Churchill had publicly doubted whether Canada could build a fleet of its own, or if it were built put it to sea, or for that matter keep it from rusting away. Nor would Britain "co-operate" with a Canadian navy—better the money be given to the Imperial mother. Such sentiments—however accurate—did not go down well. As Brooke observed, Canadians were "touchy" about criticism. But Brooke didn't broadcast his opinions, although he did betray his sympathies about Laurier's programme to his mother: "I don't trust his policy, because I don't believe he *really* wants to pay anything in any form towards the Navy. He's very French in his sympathies."

MONTREAL AND OTTAWA

MY American friends were full of kindly scorn when I announced that I was going to Canada. "A country without a soul!" they cried, and pressed books upon me, to befriend me through that Philistine bleakness. Their commiseration unnerved me, but I was heartened by a feeling that I was, in a sense, going home, and by the romance of journeying. There was romance in the long grim American train, in the great lake we passed in the blackest of nights, and could just see glinting behind dark trees; in the negro car-attendant; in the boy who perpetually cried: "Pea-nuts! Candy!" up and down the long carriages; in the lofty box they put me in to sleep; and in the fat old lady who had the berth under mine, and snored shrilly the whole night through. There was almost romance, even, in the fact that after all there was no restaurant-car on the train; and, having walked all day in the country, I dined off an orange.

I suppose an Englishman in another country, if he is simple enough, is continually and alternately struck by two thoughts: "How like England this is!" and "How unlike England this is!" When I had woken next morning, and, lying on my back, had got inside my clothes with a series of fish-like jumps, I found myself looking with startled eyes out of the window at the largest river I had ever seen. It was blue, and sunlit, and it curved spaciously. But beyond that we ran into the squalider parts of a city. It became immediately obvious that we were not in New York or Boston or any of the more orderly, the rather foreign, cities of America. There was something in the untidiness of those grimy houses, the smoky disorder of the backyards, that ran a thrill of nostalgia through me. I recognised the English way of doing things—with a difference that I could not define till later.

Determined to be in all ways the complete tourist, I took a rough preliminary survey of Montreal in an "observation-car". It was a large motor-wagonette, from which everything in Montreal could be seen in two hours. We were a most fortuitous band of twenty, who had elected so to see it. Our guide addressed us from the front through a small megaphone, telling us what everything was, what we were to be interested in, what to overlook, what to admire. He seemed the exact type of a spiritual pastor and master, shepherding his stolid and perplexed flock on a regulated path through the dust and clatter of the world. And the great hollow device out of which our instruction proceeded was so perfectly a blind mouth. I had never understood *Lycidas* before. We were sheepish enough, and fairly hungry. However, we were excellently fed. "On the right, ladies and gentlemen, is the Bank of Montreal; on the left the Presbyterian Church of St. Andrew's; on the right, again, the well-designed residence of Sir Blank Blank; further on, on the same side, the Art Museum. . . . " The outcome of it all was a vague general impression that Montreal consists of banks and churches. The people of this city spend much of their time in laying up their riches in this world or the next. Indeed, the British part of Montreal is dominated by the Scotch race; there is a Scotch spirit sensible in the whole place—in the rather narrow, rather gloomy streets, the solid, square, grey, aggressively prosperous buildings, the general greyness of the city, the air of dour prosperity. Even the Canadian habit of loading the streets with heavy telephone wires, supported by frequent black poles, seemed to increase the atmospheric resemblance to Glasgow.

But besides all this there is a kind of restraint in the air, due, perhaps, to a state of affairs which, more than any other, startles the ordinary ignorant English visitor. The average man in England has an idea of Canada as a young-eyed daughter State, composed of millions of wheat-growers and backwoodsmen of British race. It surprises him to learn that more than a quarter of the population is of French descent, that many of them cannot speak English, that they control a province, form the majority in the biggest city in Canada, and are a perpetual complication in the national politics. Even a stranger who knows this is startled at the complete separateness of the two races. Inter-marriage is very rare. They do not meet socially; only on business, and that not often. In the same city these two communities dwell side by side, with different traditions, different languages, different ideals, without sympathy or comprehension. The French in Canada are entirely devoted to—some say under the thumb of—the Roman Catholic Church. They seem like a piece of the Middle Ages, dumped after a trans-secular journey into a quite uncompromising example of our commercial time. Some of their leaders are said to have dreams of a French Republic—or theocracy—on the banks of the St. Lawrence. How this, or any other, solution of the problem is to come about, no man knows. Racial difficulties are the most enduring of all. The French and British in Canada seem to have behaved with quite extraordinary generosity and kindliness towards each other. No one is to blame. But it is not in human nature that two communities should live side by side, pretending they are one, without some irritation and mutual loss of strength. There is no open strife. But "incidents", and the memory of incidents, bear continual witness to the truth of the situation. And racial disagreement is at the bottom, often unconsciously, of many political and social movements. Sir Wilfrid Laurier performed a miracle. But no one of French birth will ever again be Premier of Canada.

Montreal and Eastern Canada suffer from that kind of ill-health which afflicts men who are cases of "double personality"—debility and spiritual paralysis. The "progressive" British-Canadian man of commerce is comically desperate of peasants who *will not* understand that increase of imports and volume of trade and numbers of millionaires are the measures of a city's greatness; and to his eye the Roman Catholic Church, with her invaluable ally Ignorance, keeps up her incessant war against the general good of the community of which she is part. So things remain.

I made my investigations in Montreal. I have to report that the Discobolus is very well, and, nowadays, looks the whole world in the face, almost quite unabashed. West of Montreal, the country seems to take on a rather more English appearance. There is still a French admixture. But the little houses are not purely Gallic, as they are along the Lower St. Lawrence; and once or twice I detected real hedges.

Ottawa came as a relief after Montreal. There is no such sense of strain and tightness in the atmosphere. The British, if not greatly in the majority, are in the ascendency; also, the city seems conscious of other than financial standards, and quietly, with dignity, aware of her own purpose. The Canadians, like the Americans, chose to have for their capital a city which did not lead in population or in wealth. This is particularly fortunate in Canada, an extremely individualistic country, whose inhabitants are only just beginning to be faintly conscious of their nationality. Here, at least, Canada is more than the Canadian. A man desiring to praise Ottawa would begin to do so without statistics of wealth and the growth of population; and this can be said of no other city in Canada except Quebec. Not that there are not immense lumber-mills and the rest in Ottawa. But the Government farm, and the Parliament Buildings, are more important. Also, although the "spoils" system obtains a good deal in this country, the nucleus of the Civil Service is much the same as in England; so there is an atmosphere of Civil Servants about Ottawa, an atmosphere of safeness and honour and massive buildings and well-shaded walks. After all, there is in the qualities of Civility and Service much beauty, of a kind which would adorn Canada.

Parliament Buildings stand finely on a headland of cliff some 160 feet above the river. There are gardens about them; and beneath, the wooded rocks go steeply down to the water. It is a position of natural boldness and significance. The buildings were put up in the middle of last century, an unfortunate period. But they have dignity, especially of line; and when evening hides their colour, and the western sky and the river take on the lovely hues of a Canadian sunset, and the lights begin to come out in the city, they seem to have the majesty and calm of a natural crown of the river-headland. The Government have bought the ground along the cliff for half a mile on either side, and propose to build all their offices there. So, in the end, if they build well, the river-front at Ottawa will be a noble sight. And—just to show that it is Canada, and not Utopia—the line of national buildings will always be broken by an expensive and superb hotel the Canadian Pacific Railway has been allowed to erect on the twin and neighbouring promontory to that of the Houses of Parliament.

The streets of Ottawa are very quiet, and shaded with trees. The houses are mostly of that cool, homely, wooden kind, with verandahs, on which, or on the steps, the whole family may sit in the evening and observe the passers-by. This is possible for both the rich and the poor, who live nearer each other in Ottawa than in most cities. In general there is an air of civilisation, which

extends even over the country round. But in the country
you see little signs, a patch of swamp, or thickets of still
untouched primaeval wood, which remind you that
Europeans have not long had this land. I was taken in a
motor-car some twenty miles or more over the execrable
roads round here, to a lovely little lake in the hills
north-west of Ottawa. We went by little French villages
and fields at first, and then through rocky, tangled
woods of birch and poplar, rich with milk-weed and
blue cornflowers, and the aromatic thimbleberry blos-
som, and that romantic, light, purple-red flower which is
called fireweed, because it is the first vegetation to
spring up in the prairie after a fire has passed over, and
so might be adopted as the emblematic flower of a sense
of humour. They told me, casually, that there was nothing but a few villages between me and the North Pole.
It is probably true of several commonly frequented
places in this country. But it gives a thrill to hear it.

But what Ottawa leaves in the mind is a certain
graciousness—dim, for it expresses a barely materialised
national spirit—and the sight of kindly English-looking
faces, and the rather lovely sound of the soft Canadian
accent, in the streets.

QUEBEC
AND THE SAGUENAY

THE boat starts from Montreal one evening, and lands you in Quebec at six next morning. The evening I left was a dull one. Heavy sulphurous clouds hung low over the city, drifting very slowly and gloomily out across the river. Mount Royal crouched, black and sullen, in the background, its crest occluded by the darkness, appearing itself a cloud materialised, resting on earth. The harbour was filled with volumes of smoke, purple and black, wreathing and sidling eastwards, from steamers and chimneys. The gigantic elevators and other harbour buildings stood mistily in this inferno, their heads clear and sinister above the mirk. It was impossible to decide whether an enormous mass of pitchy and Tartarian gloom was being slowly moulded by diabolic invisible hands into a city, or a city, the desperate and damned abode of a loveless race, was disintegrating into its proper fume and dusty chaos. With relief we turned outwards to the nobility of the St. Lawrence and the gathering dark.

On the boat I fell in with another wanderer, an American Jew, and we joined our fortunes, rather loosely, for a few days. He was one of those men whom it is a life-long pleasure to remember. I can record his existence the more easily that there is not the slightest chance of his ever reading these lines. He was a fat, large man of forty-five, obviously in business, and probably of a mediocre success. His eyes were light-coloured, very small, always watery, and perpetually roving. The lower part of his face was clean-shaven and very broad; his mouth wide, with thin, moist, colourless lips; his nose fat and Hebraic. He was rather bald. He had respect for Montreal, because, though closed to navigation for five months in the year, it is the second busiest port on the coast. He said it had Boston skinned. The French he disliked. He thought they stood in the way of Canada's progress. His mind was even more childlike and transparent than is usual with business men. The observer could see thoughts slowly floating into it, like carp in a pond. When they got near the surface, by a purely automatic process they found utterance. He was almost completely unconscious of an audience. Everything he thought of he said. He told me that his boots were giving in the sole, but would probably last this trip. He said he had not washed his feet for eight days; and that his clothes were shabby (which was true), but would do for Canada. It was interesting to see how Canada presented herself to that mind. He seemed to regard her as a kind of Boeotia, and terrifyingly dour. "These Canadian waiters," he said, "they jes' *fling* the food in y'r face. Kind'er gets yer sick, doesn't it?" I agreed. There was a Yorkshire mechanic, too, who had been in Canada four years, and preferred it to England, "because you've room to breathe", but also found that Canada had not yet learnt social comfort, and regretted the manners of "the Old Country".

We woke to find ourselves sweeping round a high cliff, at six in the morning, with a lively breeze, the river very blue and broken into ripples, and a lot of little white clouds in the sky. The air was full of gaiety and sunshine and the sense of the singing of birds, though actually, I think, there were only a few gulls crying. It was the perfection of a summer morning, thrilling with a freshness which, the fancy said, was keener than any the old world knew. And high and grey and serene above the morning lay the citadel of Quebec.

Is there any city in the world that stands so nobly as Quebec? The citadel crowns a headland, three hundred feet high, that juts boldly out into the St. Lawrence. Up to it, up the side of the hill, clambers the city, houses and steeples and huts, piled one on the other. It has the individuality and the pride of a city where great things have happened, and over which many years have passed. Quebec is as refreshing and as definite after the other cities of this continent as an immortal among a crowd of stockbrokers. She has, indeed, the radiance and repose of an immortal; but she wears her immortality youthfully. When you get among the streets of Quebec, the mediaeval, precipitous, narrow, winding, and perplexed streets, you begin to realise her charm. She almost incurs the charge of quaintness (abhorrent quality!); but even quaintness becomes attractive in this country. You are in a foreign land, for the people have an alien tongue, short stature, the quick, decided, cinematographic quality of movement, and the inexplicable cheerfulness, which mark a foreigner. You might almost be in Siena or some old German town, except that Quebec has her street-cars and grain-elevators to show that she is living.

The American Jew and I took a *calèche*, a little two-wheeled local carriage, driven by a lively Frenchman with a factitious passion for death-spots and churches. A small black and white spaniel followed the *calèche*, yapping. The American's face shone with interest. "That dawg's Michael," he said, "the hotel dawg. He's a queer little dawg. I kicked his face; and he tried to bite me. Hup, Michael!" And he laughed hoarsely. "Non!" said the driver suddenly, "it is not the 'otel dog." The American did not lose interest. "These little dawgs are all alike," he said. "Dare say if you kicked that dawg in the face, he'd bite you. Hup, Michael!" With that he fell into deep thought.

We rattled up and down the steep streets, out among tidy fields, and back into the noisily sedate city again. We saw where Wolfe fell, where Montcalm fell, where Montgomery fell. Children played where the tides of war had ebbed and flowed. Mr. Norman Angell and his friends tell us that trade is superseding war; and pacifists declare that for the future countries will win their pride or shame from commercial treaties and tariffs and bounties, and no more from battles and sieges. And there is a part of Canadian patriotism that has progressed this way. But I wonder if the hearts of that remarkable race, posterity, will ever beat the harder when they are told, "Here Mr. Borden stood when he decided to double the duty on agricultural implements," or even "In this room Mr. Ritchie conceived the plan of removing the shilling on wheat." When that happens, Quebec will be a forgotten ruin.... The reverie was broken by my friend struggling to his feet and standing, unsteady and bareheaded, in the swaying carriage. In that position he burst hoarsely into a song that I recognised as "The Star-Spangled Banner". We were passing the American Consulate. His song over, he settled down and fell into a deep sleep, and the *calèche* jolted down even narrower streets, curiously paved with planks, and ways that led through and under the ancient, tottering wooden houses.

But Quebec is too real a city to be "seen" in such a manner. And a better way of spending a few days, or years, is to sit on Dufferin Terrace, with the old Lower Town sheer beneath you, and the river beyond it, and the citadel to the right, a little above, and the Isle of Orleans and the French villages away down-stream to your left. Hour by hour the colours change, and sunlight follows shadow, and mist rises, and smoke drifts across. And through the veil of the shifting of lights and hues there remains visible the majesty of the most glorious river in the world.

From this contemplation, and from musing on men's agreement to mark by this one great sign of the Taking of the Heights of Quebec, the turning of one of the greatest currents in our history, I was torn by a journey I had been advised to make. The boat goes some hundred and thirty miles down the St. Lawrence, turns up a northern tributary, the Saguenay, goes as far as Chicoutimi, ninety miles up, and returns to Quebec. Both on this trip, and between Quebec and Montreal, we touched at many little French villages, by day and by night. Their *habitants*, the French-Canadian peasants, are a jolly sight. They are like children in their noisy content. They are poor and happy, Roman Catholics; they laugh a great deal; and they continually sing. They do not progress at all. As a counter to these admirable people we had on our boat a great many priests. They diffused an atmosphere of black, of unpleasant melancholy. Their faces had that curiously unwashed look, and were for the most part of a mean and very untrustworthy expression. Their eyes were small, shifty, and cruel, and would not meet the gaze....The choice between our own age and mediaeval times is a very hard one.

It was almost full night when we left the twenty-mile width of the St. Lawrence, and turned up a gloomy inlet. By reason of the night and of comparison with the river from which we had come, this stream appeared unnaturally narrow. Darkness hid all detail, and we were only aware of vast cliffs, sometimes dense with trees, sometimes bare faces of sullen rock. They shut us in, oppressively, but without heat. There are no banks to this river, for the most part; only these walls, rising sheer from the water to the height of two thousand feet, going down sheer beneath it, or rather by the side of it, to many times that depth. The water was of some colour blacker than black. Even by daylight it is inky and sinister. It flows without foam or ripple. No white showed in the wake of the boat. The ominous shores were without sign of life, save for a rare light every few miles, to mark some bend in the chasm. Once a canoe with two Indians shot out of the shadows, passed under our stern, and vanished silently down stream. We all became hushed and apprehensive. The night was gigantic and terrible. There were a few stars, but the flood slid along too swiftly to reflect them. The whole scene seemed some Stygian imagination of Dante. As we drew further and further into that lightless land, little twists and curls of vapour wriggled over the black river-surface. Our homeless, irrelevant, tiny steamer seemed to hang between two abysms. One became suddenly aware of the miles of dark water beneath. I found that under a prolonged gaze the face of the river began to writhe and eddy, as if from some horrible suppressed emotion. It seemed likely that something might appear. I reflected that if the river failed us, all hope was gone; and that anyhow this region was the abode of devils. I went to bed.

Next day we steamed down the river again. By daylight some of the horror goes, but the impression of ancientness and desolation remains. The gloomy flood is entirely shut in by the rock or the tangled pine and birch forests of these great cliffs, except in one or two places, where a chine and a beach have given lodging to lonely villages. One of these is at the end of a long bay, called Ha-Ha Bay. The local guide-book, an early example of the school of fantastic realism so popular among our younger novelists, says that this name arose from the "laughing ejaculations" of the early French explorers, who had mistaken this lengthy blind-alley for the main stream. "Ha! Ha!" they said. So like an early explorer.

At the point where the Saguenay joins the St. Lawrence, here twenty miles wide, I "stopped off" for a day, to feel the country more deeply. The village is called

Tadousac, and consists of an hotel and French fishermen, to whom Quebec is a distant, unvisited city of legend. The afternoon was very hot. I wandered out along a thin margin of yellow sand to the extreme rocky point where the waters of the two rivers meet and swirl. There I lay, and looked at the strange humps of the Laurentian hills, and the dark green masses of the woods, impenetrable depths of straight and leaning and horizontal trees, broken here and there by great bald granite rocks, and behind me the little village, where the earliest church in Canada stands. Away in the St. Lawrence there would be a flash as an immense white fish jumped. Miles out an occasional steamer passed, bound to England perhaps. And once, hugging the coast, came a half-breed paddling a canoe with a small diamond-shaped sail, filled with trout. The cliff above me was crowned with beds of blue flowers, whose names I did not know. Against the little gulfs and coasts of rock at my feet were washing a few white logs of driftwood. I wondered if they could have floated across from England, or if they could be from the *Titanic*. The sun was very hot, the sky a clear light blue, almost cloudless, like an English sky, and the water seemed fairly deep. I stripped, hovered a while on the brink, and plunged. The current was unexpectedly strong. I seemed to feel that two-mile-deep body of black water moving against me. And it was cold as death. Stray shreds of the St. Lawrence water were warm and cheerful. But the current of the Saguenay, on such a day, seemed unnaturally icy. As my head came up I made one dash for the land, scrambled out on the hot rocks, and lay there panting. Then I dried on a handkerchief, dressed, and ran back home, still shivering, through the woods to the hotel.

1.   Montreal Harbour, 1908. *Archives of Ontario.*

*You'll be pleased to know I'm looking round the Empire, won't
you? Rather in your line. . . . But they're a rough lot Hugh.
Their manners.
But you should hear me sob when they speak of The Old
Country. As they continually do. . . . And I am expert at singing
"O, Canada!" in English and French.*

From a postcard to Hugh Dalton, [Quebec], 5 July 1913.

2. Jacques Cartier Market, Montreal, 1906. *Archives of Ontario.*

Quebec   Chateau Frontenac.

3. Chateau Frontenac, from Dufferin Terrace, Quebec City, c.1913.
Brooke Archive, King's College, Cambridge.

4.   Chateau Frontenac, lower town and harbour, Quebec City,
n.d. *Public Archives of Canada.*

Is there any city in the world that stands so nobly as Quebec?
The citadel crowns a headland, three hundred feet high, that juts
boldly into the St. Lawrence. Up to it, up the side of the hill,
clambers the city, houses and steeples and huts, piled one on the
other. It has the individuality and pride of a city where great
things have happened, and over which many years have passed.
Quebec is as refreshing and as definite after the other cities of
this continent as an immortal among a crowd of stockbrokers.

From "Quebec and the Saguenay".

5.   Champlain Market, Quebec City, c. 1911.
Public Archives of Canada.

6. Near Tadoussac, Quebec, 1912. *Archives of Ontario.*

7. Hotel Tadoussac, Tadoussac, Quebec, c. 1912.
Public Archives of Canada.

I stopped here for a day or two, & I'm glad I did. I'm sick of large towns, this is a small wee seaside resort, just a village, no railway & a steamer a day. A large hotel & cottages. It's at the corner where the Saguenay flows into the St. Lawrence—& such a lovely place, & I'm so peaceful & happy—& this afternoon I stole out & bathed—it was cold water & lay on the rocks & composed a Hymn. . . . It's rather nice being entirely unconnected & planless.

From a letter to Cathleen Nesbitt, 3 July 1913.

8. Approaching Trinity and Eternity, Saguenay River, c. 1910.
Public Archives of Canada.

The whole scene seemed some Stygian imagination of Dante. As
we drew further and further into that lightless land, little twists
and curls of vapour wriggled over the black river-surface. Our
harmless, irrelevant, tiny steamer seemed to hang between two
abysms. One became suddenly aware of the miles of dark water
beneath. I found that under a prolonged gaze the face of the
river began to writhe and eddy, as if from some horrible
suppressed emotion. It seemed likely that something might
appear. I reflected that if the river failed us, all hope was gone;
and that anyhow this region was the abode of devils.
I went to bed.

From "Quebec and the Saguenay".

9. Ottawa. Rupert Brooke with the Scott family and friends in Scott's garden. *Scott Papers, Thomas Fisher Library, University of Toronto.*

I had been told by [John Masefield] that he knew (by correspondence) the Canadian poet Duncan Campbell Scott. So I looked him up & introduced myself & he & his wife were very kind & "took me up", & gave me letters on here & elsewhere & introduced me to everybody. He's about fifty & head of the Indian affairs in the civil service. They had one daughter who died six years ago, a child & it smashed them up rather. Also he leads rather a lonely life from the literary point of view, for there's hardly anybody he can talk to about such things. So I can think without vanity—he liked to see me.

From a letter to his mother, Ottawa, July 1913.

II

FORTIFIED with letters of introduction from Duncan Campbell Scott, Brooke moved into Ontario. He immediately felt more at home—"after the States and after Quebec it is English". He even claimed to see "a hedge or two", and noted the characteristic orderliness of the soft Ontario countryside: "Men have lived contentedly on this land and died where they were born, and so given it a certain sanctity." At the time most Ontarians would have applauded that sentiment, for it was largely true. Old Ontario, that unique blend of city and country, of prosperous farms, of small cities and towns with luxuriant, productive hinterlands was at its apogee. It pleased Brooke, but despite its aggressive Britishness (resurgent in 1912 and 1913 because of the centennial of the War of 1812) he would have rejected it utterly had he gotten to know its cloying provincialism, its staunch, unbending protestantism, and its fierce fondness for temperance in all things (and especially booze). Brooke travelled from Ottawa to Prescott by train, and then he took a lake steamer for the trip to Toronto.

Scott's letters were to Edmund Morris (a celebrated painter whose reputation rested chiefly on his work with Indians), to Sir John Willison (intimate of Wilfrid Laurier, one-time editor of the Toronto *Globe* and in 1913 Canadian correspondent for *The Times*), and to Newton McTavish (editor of the then influential *Canadian Magazine*, a journal of the arts that frequently published Scott's verse). Besides the literary contacts, Scott provided Brooke with an open letter to all western Indian agents.

Brooke called on Edmund Morris first, and was immediately taken round for lunch at the Arts and Letters Club, five years old and the centre of Canadian literary and cultural life. The nucleus that would form the Group of Seven met in the club's rooms, then situated in the old Assizes building, off the Court House on Adelaide Street. So did critics like Hector Charlesworth of *Saturday Night* magazine, later the group's most persistent and vociferous detractor. Today all that remains from those lively, even vituperative days is the stricture against female members.

Nearly twenty years after Rupert's visit R. H. Hathaway, the Canadian bibliophile and club member, wrote about it for the American collector's journal, *The Colophon*:

> The luncheon attendance at the Arts and Letters Club on the day Brooke made his first appearance there was scant, for the time being late July, all the Club members who could get away had hied themselves to Muskoka or Georgian Bay or elsewhere to escape the heat, which as I remember, was terrific. I thus had a notable opportunity to study our unusual-looking visitor, for unusual-looking he was in the fullest sense of the term. He seemed to me, indeed, to be the most beautiful youth—the word beautiful, used in this connection may seem somewhat extravagant, but I use it advisedly—that I had ever seen. Rather above medium height, straight, slim, with remarkably well-cut features, clear blue eyes, the coloring of a girl, and a mass of fine, golden-brown hair, worn rather long, he looked the veritable picture of a young Greek god—of Apollo himself. There was nothing of the effeminate about him for all the slightness of his figure and the delicacy of his coloring; indeed, one felt instinctively that he was no stranger to the cricket-bat or the oar. Men as a rule pay little attention to other men's clothes, but I recall that Brooke wore a dark grey suit which looked as if it had seen good service, and that his wide-brimmed soft felt hat, tossed on a table behind the one at which he sat, also spoke of usage. In fact, one of the Club members, speaking of our visitor later, referred to him as 'the man with the shabby clothes.' His appearance, altogether, was

such as to incline one at once to set him down as a poet or a painter or a musician—and the big loose-knotted tie which he wore definitely decided the matter....

Brooke was quiet and undemonstrative in his bearing, and appeared to be entirely free from side or eccentricities of any kind, his only mannerisms, so far as I can recall, being occasionally to run the fingers of a long, finely-shaped hand through his mass of soft hair, which was parted not quite in the center, and to shake back the long locks when, now and again, they would fall over his high, broad brow.

There can be no doubt that, in the company of intimates, the poet was a companion of companions, for he revealed himself as the possessor of a ready, alert mind, a keen sense of humor and a quick wit, this last with a tinge—or more than a tinge—of the satirical in it; but I found him to be anything but communicative. He seemed, indeed, while graciousness itself, to be the characteristic Englishman, reserved, if not shy, seldom speaking unless in response to a direct question or to ask a question of his own. It may be that this was because he felt lonely in consequence of his long distance from home; but I have a suspicion that Brooke had himself in mind when he wrote as follows in the chapter of his *Letters from America* headed 'Ontario', describing his journey up Lake Ontario to Toronto by steamer: 'But the English sat quite still, looking straight in front of them, thinking of nothing at all, and hoping that nobody would speak to them.'...

Brooke, I remember, said that he and his fellows most looked up to Robert Bridges, as had been evidenced by the dedication of the then recently published (December 1912) first volume of *Georgian Poetry* to him. They had also, he said, a high regard for William Butler Yeats. But Kipling and Noyes, for all their popularity, apparently did not count with Brooke and the other 'Georgians', as he would not speak of them.

Brooke admitted, in answer to a question, that he didn't know much about the work of our Canadian poets, but he said he had read some things by Bliss Carman and others and liked them, and he intimated that he intended to find out more about what was being done by the Canadians....

All these statements and admissions, as I have intimated, had almost to be dragged out of Brooke. But he showed himself eager to learn what he could about Canada and things Canadian, and particularly about Western Canada, where he seemed, from his questions, to expect to find the Indian in something like his aboriginal state.

I walked back with Brooke from the Club to his hotel on the last day of his stay in Toronto, beguiling the way by imparting such banal information as that Toronto was the second largest city in the Dominion, that the then recently completed C.P.R. building, towering ahead of us, was the tallest structure in the Empire, and so on. His mind, however, seems to have been busy with other matters, for when I shook hands with him and bade him goodbye and good-luck, he remarked that he was going to his room to write a poem. I have often wondered whether he succeeded in writing that poem, but I have never been able to find a definite clue to it in his published work.

The poem Brooke wrote was "Doubts", first titled "To Cathleen", and quickly shipped off to her, without an accompanying letter.

> When she sleeps, her soul, I know,
> Goes a wanderer on the air,
> Wings where I may never go,
> Leaves her lying, still and fair,
> Waiting, empty, laid aside,
> Like a dress upon a chair. . . .
> This I know, and yet I know
> Doubts that will not be denied.
>
> For if the soul be not in place,
> What has laid trouble in her face?
> And, sits there nothing ware and wise
> Behind the curtains of her eyes,
> What is it, in the self's eclipse,
> Shadows, soft and passingly,
> About the corners of her lips,
> The smile that is essential she?
>
> And if the spirit be not there,
> Why is fragrance in the hair?

"Doubts" the poem might have been called, but there is no doubt that Rupert was fully on the mend—physically and psychologically from his collapse the year before. The best he had managed on his journey thus far had been bits of sharp, amusing, but more often clever doggerel. "Doubts", for all its reminiscences of John Donne, was evidence of Brooke reclaiming his health.

Brooke left his own impression of the Arts and Letters Club in a letter to Edward Marsh:

I've found here an Arts and Letters Club of poets, painters, journalists, etc., where they'd heard of me and read G. P. [Georgian Poetry], and Oh, Eddie, one fellow actually possessed my *Poems*. Awful Triumph. Every now and then one comes up and presses my hand, and says, 'Wal, Sir, you can not know what a memorable Day in my life this is.' Then I do my boyish-modesty stunt and go pink all over; and everyone thinks it *too* delightful. One man says to me, 'Mr. Brooks (my Canadian name), Sir, I must tell you that in my opinion you have Mr. Noyes skinned.' This means that I'm better than him; a great compliment.

Frequently in letters to his English friends Brooke paraded the Canadians as amiable rustics. It was a pose they expected from him. Yet he really was complimented and complimentary about his time at the Arts and Letters Club of Toronto. He concluded his letter to Marsh, "But they're really a quite up-to-date lot, and very cheery and pleasant. I go tomorrow to the desert & the wilds."

Shortly after Brooke's departure from Toronto, Hathaway was asked by Lindsay Crawford, editor of the *Globe*'s Saturday Magazine Section to recall the poet's visit and write something about his poetry. Hathaway prided himself that his article was the "first 'appreciation' of Brooke to make its appearance in print". It appeared in the *Globe* on 2 August 1913:

Mr. Rupert Brooke, a Fellow of King's College, Cambridge, is at present on a tour of Canada, studying social and political conditions, as the special correspondent of *The Westminster Gazette*. Mr. Brooke, who was in Toronto for a few days last week, is one of the most remarkable of the young men who are rapidly bringing poetry into her own in England. As yet he has but one book to his credit—*Poems*, published in 1911—but that one book, on its appearance, established Mr. Brooke's position firmly among the so-called 'Georgian' poets, the critics hailing it, almost with united voice, as one of the most original and remarkable first books of poems issued in many a day.

A white-flashing radiance, a high, clear, starry light, is the distinguishing thing about Mr. Brooke's work, though he can be vividly realistic when in the mood. His is, in all truth, no imitative school muse. That clear-burning, swift-moving light of his did not come through reading or study; it is his own, the gift of the high gods themselves. Nor is that flashing light cold and brilliant like the far stars, bright and clear though it is; we feel the man as well as the poet behind and in Mr. Brooke's poems. These, in a word, are no mere exercises; they are living things, for the writer found them in his heart.

In technique Mr. Brooke's work is as remarkable as it is in substance. He shows a liking for the sonnet, and that he is at home in that difficult form of verse is plainly shown by the example given below, which begins his *Poems*. The unexpected conclusion of this sonnet is quite characteristic of Mr. Brooke's poems, many of them taking just such a sudden and unlooked-for turn at the end. But though the straightjacket nature of the sonnet is no doubt good discipline for him, Mr. Brooke's best work is in a free, semi-blank verse, marked by unexpected rhythms and subtle harmonies which delight the attentive ear.

That Mr. Brooke will go far, provided that he can resist the things which beset the way of the young man of genius, is a safe prediction; at any rate, the future of this modest, fresh-faced lad—he is but twenty-five—will be watched with real interest by those who were so fortunate as to meet him while he was in Toronto last week.

Dust

When the white flame in us is gone,
    And we that lost the world's delight
Stiffen in darkness, left alone
    To crumble in our separate night;

When your swift hair is quiet in death,
    And through the lips corruption thrust
Has stilled the labour of my breath—
    When we are dust, when we are dust!—

Not dead, not undesirous yet,
    Still sentient, still unsatisfied,
We'll ride the air, and shine, and flit,
    Around the places where we died,

And dance as dust before the sun,
    And light of foot, and unconfined,
Hurry from road to road, and run
    About the errands of the wind.

And every mote, on earth or air,
  Will speed and gleam, down later days,
And like a secret pilgrim fare
  By eager and invisible ways,

Nor ever rest, nor ever lie,
  Till, beyond thinking, out of view,
One mote of all the dust that's I
  Shall meet one atom that was you.

Then in some garden hushed from wind,
  Warm in a sunset's afterglow,
The lovers in the flowers will find
  A sweet and strange unquiet grow

Upon the peace; and, past desiring,
  So high a beauty in the air,
And such a light, and such a quiring,
  And such a radiant ecstasy there,

They'll know not if it's fire, or dew,
  Or out of earth, or in the height,
Singing, or flame, or scent, or hue,
  Or two that pass, in light, to light,

Out of the garden higher, higher....
  But in that instant they shall learn
The shattering ecstasy of our fire,
  And the weak passionless hearts will burn

And faint in that amazing glow,
  Until the darkness close above;
Until they will know—poor fools, they'll know!—
  One moment, what it is to love.

In November 1913 Brooke wrote to Hathaway from Suva, Fiji in the South Pacific to thank him for "that kind, that too kind" article. "I won't discuss it," he said uncharacteristically, "though I won't pretend that praise of my poetry doesn't make me feel warm."

Like most English visitors Brooke was determined to see Niagara Falls; he was equally determined *not* to be impressed. He wrote to his old friend at King's, A. F. Scholfield, on paper wet with spray from the falls:

There is romance for you! A letter dewy with Niagara read by
a corpulent turbaned rajah of a librarian under the deodars of

Taj Mahal. (Local Colour.) But it shows you what the British
Empire is! (I am become (1) a strong Imperialist, (2) a rabid
anti-Canadian, (3) a *violent* Englander). But, o Scho. I'm so
impressed by Niagara. I hoped not to be. But I horribly am.
The colour of the water, the strength of it, and the clouds of
spray—I'm afraid I'm a Victorian at heart after all. Please don't
breathe a word of it; I want to keep such shreds of reputation
as I have left. Yet it's true. For I sit and stare at the thing and
have the purest Nineteenth Century grandiose thoughts, about
the Destiny of Man, the Irresistibility of Fate, the Doom of
Nations, the fact that Death awaits us All, and so forth. Wordsworth Redivivus. Oh dear! Oh dear!

So, duly having been conquered by Niagara, Brooke set
out for the "desert & the wilds". He meant the fertile Canadian prairies about which he must have known something, if
only from advertisements. First Laurier's Liberal government
and then Robert Borden's Tories had smothered Britain with
reams of propaganda about the last, best west. They claimed
the prairies were a British farmer's or labourer's dream and
said so with enough force that H. H. Asquith, the British
Prime Minister and Brooke's friend, denounced emigration
and pleaded for English farmers to stay at home.

For a few years it had seemed as though Laurier's 1901
boast that the twentieth would be "Canada's Century" might
become a reality. But by the time Brooke saw the west
prosperity had come and gone. Canada and particularly the
west faced a sharp recession in the summer of 1913. Money
had dried up and the fabulous land boom was largely over
although few of the boosters Rupert met chose to comment
on it.

ONTARIO

THE great joy of travelling in Canada is to do it by water. The advantage of this is that you can keep fairly clean and quiet of nerves; the disadvantage is that you don't "see the country". I travelled most of the way from Ottawa to Toronto by water. But between Ottawa and Prescott then, and later from Toronto to Niagara Falls, and thence to Sarnia, there is a good deal of Southern Ontario to be seen—the part which has counted as Ontario so far. And I saw it through a faint grey-pink mist of *Heimweh*. For after the States and after Quebec it is English. There are weather-beaten farm-houses, rolling country, thickets of trees, little hills green and grey in the distance, decorous small fields, orchards, and, I swear, a hedge or two. Most of the towns we went through are a little too vivacious or too pert to be European. But there seemed to be real villages occasionally, and the land had a quiet air of occupation. Men have lived contentedly on this land and died where they were born, and so given it a certain sanctity. Away north the wild begins, and is only now being brought into civilisation, inhabited, made productive, explored, and exploited. But this country has seen the generations pass, and won something of that repose and security which countries acquire from the sight.

The wise traveller from Ottawa to Toronto catches a boat at Prescott, and puffs judicially between two nations up the St. Lawrence and across Lake Ontario. We were a cosmopolitan, middle-class bunch (it is the one distinction between the Canadian and American languages that Canadians tend to say "bunch" but Americans "crowd"), out to enjoy the scenery. For this stretch of the river is notoriously picturesque, containing the Thousand Isles. The Thousand Isles vary from six inches to hundreds of yards in diameter. Each, if big enough, has been bought by a rich man—generally an American—who has built a castle on it. So the whole isn't much more beautiful than Golder's Green. We picked our way carefully between the islands. The Americans on board sat in rows saying, "That house was built by Mr. ____. Made his money in biscuits. Cost three hundred thousand dollars, e-recting that building. Yessir." The Canadians sat looking out the other way, and said, "In 1910 this land was worth twenty thousand an acre; now it's worth forty-five thousand. Next year...." and their eyes grew solemn as the eyes of men who think deep and holy thoughts. But the English sat quite still, looking straight in front of them, thinking of nothing at all, and hoping that nobody would speak to them. So we fared; until, well on in the afternoon, we came to the entrance of Lake Ontario.

There is something ominous and unnatural about these great lakes. The sweet flow of a river, and the unfriendly restless vitality of the sea, men may know and love. And the little lakes we have in Europe are but as fresh-water streams that have married and settled down, alive and healthy and comprehensible. Rivers (except the Saguenay) are human. The sea, very properly, will not be allowed in heaven. It has no soul. It is unvintageable, cruel, treacherous, what you will. But, in the end—while we have it with us—it is all right; even though that all-rightness result but, as with France, from the recognition of an age-long feud and an irremediable lack of sympathy. But these monstrous lakes, which ape the ocean, are not proper to fresh water or salt. They have souls, perceptibly, and wicked ones.

We steamed out, that day, over a flat, stationary mass of water, smooth with the smoothness of metal or polished stone or one's finger-nail. There was a slight haze everywhere. The lake was a terrible dead-silver colour, the gleam of its surface shot with flecks of blue and a vapoury enamel-green. It was like a gigantic silver shield. Its glint was inexplicably sinister and dead, like the glint on glasses worn by a blind man. In front the steely mist hid the horizon, so that the occasional rock or little island and the one ship in sight seemed hung in air. They were reflected to a preternatural length in the glassy floor. Our boat appeared to leave no wake; those strange waters closed up foamlessly behind her. But our black smoke hung, away back on the trail, in a thick, clearly-bounded cloud, becalmed in the hot, windless air, very close over the water, like an evil soul after death that cannot win dissolution. Behind us and to the right lay the low, woody shores of Southern Ontario and Prince Edward Peninsula, long dark lines of green, stretching thinner and thinner, interminably, into the distance. The lake around us was dull, though the sun shone full on it. It gleamed, but without radiance.

Toronto (pronounce *T'ranto*, please) is difficult to describe. It has an individuality, but an elusive one; yet not through any queerness or difficult shade of eccentricity; a subtly normal, an indefinably obvious personality. It is a healthy, cheerful city (by modern standards); a clean-shaven, pink-faced, respectably dressed, fairly energetic, unintellectual, passably sociable, well-to-do, public-school-and-'varsity sort of city. One knows in one's own life certain bright and pleasant figures; people who occupy the nearer middle distance, unobtrusive but not negligible; wardens of the marches between acquaintanceship and friendship. It is always nice to meet them, and in parting one looks back at them once. They are,

healthily and simply, the most fitting product of a not
perfect environment; good-sorts; normal, but not too
normal; distinctly themselves, but not distinguished.
They support civilisation. You can trust them in anything, if your demand be for nothing extremely intelligent or absurdly altruistic. One of these could be exhib-
ited in any gallery in the universe, "Perfect Specimen;
Upper Middle Classes; Twentieth Century"—and we
should not be ashamed. They are not vexed by impossible dreams, nor outrageously materialistic, nor perplexed
by overmuch prosperity, nor spoilt by reverse. Souls for
whom the wind is always nor'-nor'-west, and they sail
nearer success than failure, and nearer wisdom than
lunacy. Neither leaders nor slaves—but no Tomlinsons!—
whomsoever of your friends you miss, *them* you will
certainly meet again, not unduly pardoned, the fifty-first
by the Throne.

Such is Toronto. A brisk city of getting on for half a
million inhabitants, the largest British city in Canada (in
spite of the cheery Italian faces that pop up at you out
of excavations in the street), liberally endowed with
millionaires, not lacking its due share of destitution,
misery, and slums. It is no mushroom city of the West, it
has its history; but at the same time it has grown
immensely of recent years. It is situated on the shores of
a lovely lake; but you never see that, because the railways have occupied the entire lake front. So if, at evening, you try to find your way to the edge of the water,
you are checked by a region of smoke, sheds, trucks,
wharves, storehouses, "depôts", railway-lines, signals,
and locomotives and trains that wander on the tracks up
and down and across streets, pushing their way through
the pedestrians, and tolling, as they go, in the American
fashion, an immense melancholy bell, intent, apparently,
on some private and incommunicable grief. Higher up
are the business quarters, a few sky-scrapers in the
American style without the modern American beauty,
but one of which advertises itself as the highest in the

British Empire; streets that seem less narrow than Montreal, but not unrespectably wide; "the buildings are generally substantial and often handsome" (the too kindly Herr Baedeker). Beyond that the residential part, with quiet streets, gardens open to the road, shady verandahs, and homes, generally of wood, that are a deal more pleasant to see than the houses in a modern English town.

Toronto is the centre and heart of the Province of Ontario; and Ontario, with a third of the whole population of Canada, directs the country for the present, conditioned by the French on one hand and the West on the other. And in this land, that is as yet hardly at all conscious of itself as a nation, Toronto and Ontario do their best in leading and realising national sentiment. A Toronto man, like most Canadians, dislikes an Englishman; but, unlike some Canadians, he detests an American. And he has some inkling of the conditions and responsibilities of the British Empire. The tradition is in him. His fathers fought to keep Canada British.

It is never easy to pick out of the turmoil of an election the real powers that have moved men; and it is especially difficult in a country where politics are so corrupt as they are in Canada. But certainly this British feeling helped to throw Ontario, and so the country, against Reciprocity with the United States in 1911; and it is keeping it, in the comedy of the Navy Question, on Mr. Borden's side—rather from distrust of his opponents' sincerity, perhaps, than from admiration of the fix he is in. It has been used, this patriotism, to aid the wealthy interests, which are all-powerful here; and it will continue to be a ball in the tennis of party politics. But it is real; it will remain, potential of good, among all the forces that are certain for evil.

Toronto, soul of Canada, is wealthy, busy, commercial, Scotch, absorbent of whisky; but she is duly aware of other things. She has a most modern and efficient interest in education; and here are gathered what faint,

faint beginnings or premonitions of such things as Art
Canada can boast (except the French-Canadians, who, it
is complained, produce disproportionately much literature, and waste their time on their own unprofitable
songs). Most of those few who have begun to paint the
landscape of Canada centre there, and a handful of
people who know about books. In these things, as in all,
this city is properly and cheerfully to the front. It can
scarcely be doubted that the first Repertory Theatre in
Canada will be founded in Toronto, some thirty years
hence, and will very daringly perform *Candida* and *The
Silver Box*. Canada is a live country, live, but not, like
the States, kicking. In these trifles of Art and "culture",
indeed, she is much handicapped by the proximity of
the States. For her poets and writers are apt to be drawn
thither, for the better companionship there and the
higher rates of pay.

But Toronto—Toronto is the subject. One must say
something—*what* must one say about Toronto? What can
one? What has anybody ever said? It is impossible to give
it anything but commendation. It is not squalid like
Birmingham, or cramped like Canton, or scattered like
Edmonton, or sham like Berlin, or hellish like New
York, or tiresome like Nice. It is all right. The only
depressing thing is that it will always be what it is, only
larger, and that no Canadian city can ever be anything
better or different. If they are good they may become
Toronto.

NIAGARA FALLS

SAMUEL BUTLER has a lot to answer for. But for
him, a modern traveller could spend his time peace-
fully admiring the scenery instead of feeling himself
bound to dog the simple and grotesque of the world for
the sake of their too-human comments. It is his fault if a
peasant's *naïveté* has come to outweigh the beauty of
rivers, and the remarks of clergymen are more than
mountains. It is very restful to give up all effort at
observing human nature and drawing social and political
deductions from trifles, and to let oneself relapse into
wide-mouthed worship of the wonders of nature. And
this is very easy at Niagara. Niagara means nothing. It is
not leading anywhere. It does not result from anything.
It throws no light on the effects of Protection, nor on the
Facility for Divorce in America, nor on Corruption in
Public Life, nor on Canadian character, nor even on the
Navy Bill. It is merely a great deal of water falling over
some cliffs. But it is very remarkably that. The human
race, apt as a child to destroy what it admires, has done
its best to surround the Falls with every distraction,
incongruity, and vulgarity. Hotels, powerhouses, bridges,
trams, picture post-cards, sham legends, stalls, booths,
rifle-galleries, and side-shows frame them about. And

there are Touts. Niagara is the central home and breed-
ing-place for all the touts of earth. There are touts
insinuating, and touts raucous, greasy touts, brazen
touts, and upper-class, refined, gentlemanly, take-you-
by-the-arm touts; touts who intimidate and touts who
wheedle; professionals, amateurs, and *dilettanti*, male
and female; touts who would photograph you with your
arm round a young lady against a faked background of
the sublimest cataract, touts who would bully you into
cars, char-à-bancs, elevators, or tunnels, or deceive you
into a carriage and pair, touts who would sell you picture postcards, moccasins, sham Indian beadwork, blankets, tee-pees, and crockery; and touts, finally, who have
no apparent object in the world, but just purely, simply,
merely, incessantly, indefatigably, and ineffugibly—to
tout. And in the midst of all this, overwhelming it all,
are the Falls. He who sees them instantly forgets
humanity. They are not very high, but they are over-
powering. They are divided by an island into two parts,
the Canadian and the American.

Half a mile or so above the Falls, on either side, the
water of the great stream begins to run more swiftly and
in confusion. It descends with ever-growing speed. It
begins chattering and leaping, breaking into a thousand
ripples, throwing up joyful fingers of spray. Sometimes it
is divided by islands and rocks, sometimes the eye can
see nothing but a waste of laughing, springing, foamy
waves, turning, crossing, even seeming to stand for an
instant erect, but always borne impetuously forward like
a crowd of triumphant feasters. Sit close down by it, and
you see a fragment of the torrent against the sky, mot-
tled, steely, and foaming, leaping onward in far-flung
criss-cross strands of water. Perpetually the eye is on the
point of descrying a pattern in this weaving, and perpetually it is cheated by change. In one place part of the
flood plunges over a ledge a few feet high and a quarter
of a mile or so long, in a uniform and stable curve. It

gives an impression of almost military concerted movement, grown suddenly out of confusion. But it is swiftly
lost again in the multitudinous tossing merriment. Here
and there a rock close to the surface is marked by a
white wave that faces backwards and seems to be rush-
ing madly up-stream, but is really stationary in the
headlong charge. But for these signs of reluctance, the
waters seem to fling themselves on with some foreknowl-
edge of their fate, in an ever wilder frenzy. But it is no
Maeterlinckian pre-science. They prove, rather, that
Greek belief that the great crashes are preceded by a
louder merriment and a wilder gaiety. Leaping in the
sunlight, careless, entwining, clamorously joyful, the
waves riot on towards the verge.

But there they change. As they turn to the sheer
descent, the white and blue and slate-colours, in the heart
of the Canadian Falls at least, blend and deepen to a
rich, wonderful, luminous green. On the edge of disaster
the river seems to gather herself, to pause, to lift a head
noble in ruin, and then, with a slow grandeur, to plunge
into the eternal thunder and white chaos below. Where
the stream runs shallower it is a kind of violet colour,
but both violet and green fray and frill to white as they
fall. The mass of water, striking some ever-hidden base
of rock, leaps up the whole two hundred feet again in
pinnacles and domes of spray. The spray falls back into
the lower river once more; all but a little that fines to
foam and white mist, which drifts in layers along the air,
graining it, and wanders out on the wind over the trees
and gardens and houses, and so vanishes.

The manager of one of the great power-stations on
the banks of the river above the Falls told me that the
centre of the riverbed at the Canadian Falls is deep and
of a saucer shape. So it may be possible to fill this up to
a uniform depth, and divert a lot of water for the
power-houses. And this, he said, would supply the need
for more power, which will certainly soon arise, without

taking away from the beauty of Niagara. This is a handsome concession of the utilitarians to ordinary sight-seers. Yet, I doubt if we shall be satisfied. The real secret of the beauty and terror of the Falls is not their height or width, but the feeling of colossal power and of unintelligible disaster caused by the plunge of that vast body of water. If that were taken away, there would be little visible change; but the heart would be gone.

The American Falls do not inspire this feeling in the same way as the Canadian. It is because they are less in volume, and because the water does not fall so much into one place. By comparison their beauty is almost delicate and fragile. They are extraordinarily level, one long curtain of lacework and woven foam. Seen from opposite, when the sun is on them, they are blindingly white, and the clouds of spray show dark against them. With both Falls the colour of the water is the ever-altering wonder. Greens and blues, purples and whites, melt into one another, fade, and come again, and change with the changing sun. Sometimes they are as richly diaphanous as a precious stone, and glow from within with a deep, inexplicable light. Sometimes the white intricacies of dropping foam become opaque and creamy. And always there are the rainbows. If you come suddenly upon the Falls from above, a great double rainbow, very vivid, spanning the extent of spray from top to bottom, is the first thing you see. If you wander along the cliff opposite, a bow springs into being in the American Falls, accompanies you courteously on your walk, dwindles and dies as the mist ends, and awakens again as you reach the Canadian tumult. And the bold traveller who attempts the trip under the American Falls sees, when he dare open his eyes to anything, tiny baby rainbows, some four or five yards in span, leaping from rock to rock among the foam, and gambolling beside him, barely out of hand's reach, as he goes. One I saw in that place was a complete circle, such as I have never seen before, and so near that I could put my foot on it.

It is a terrifying journey, beneath and behind the Falls.
The senses are battered and bewildered by the thunder
of the water and the assault of wind and spray; or
rather, the sound is not of falling water, but merely of
falling; a noise of unspecified ruin. So, if you are close
behind the endless clamour, the sight cannot recognise
liquid in the masses that hurl past. You are dimly and
pitifully aware that sheets of light and darkness are
falling in great curves in front of you. Dull omnipresent
foam washes the face. Farther away, in the roar and
hissing, clouds of spray seem literally to slide down
some invisible plane of air.

Beyond the foot of the Falls the river is like a slipping
floor of marble, green with veins of dirty white, made
by the scum that was foam. It slides very quietly and
slowly down for a mile or two, sullenly exhausted. Then
it turns to a dull sage green, and hurries more swiftly,
smooth and ominous. As the walls of the ravine close in,
trouble stirs, and the waters boil and eddy. These are
the lower rapids, a sight more terrifying than the Falls,
because less intelligible. Close in its bands of rock the
river surges tumultuously forward, writhing and leaping
as if inspired by a demon. It is pressed by the straits
into a visibly convex form. Great planes of water slide
past. Sometimes it is thrown up into a pinnacle of foam
higher than a house, or leaps with incredible speed from
the crest of one vast wave to another, along the shining
curve between, like the spring of a wild beast. Its motion
continually suggests muscular action. The power mani-
fest in these rapids moves one with a different sense of
awe and terror from that of the Falls. Here the inhuman
life and strength are spontaneous, active, almost reso-
lute; masculine vigour compared with the passive gigantic power, female, helpless and overwhelming, of the
Falls. A place of fear.

One is drawn back, strangely, to a contemplation of
the Falls, at every hour, and especially by night, when
the cloud of spray becomes an immense visible ghost,

straining and wavering high above the river, white and pathetic and translucent. The Victorian lies very close below the surface in every man. There one can sit and let great cloudy thoughts of destiny and the passage of empires drift through the mind; for such dreams are at home by Niagara. I could not get out of my mind the thought of a friend, who said that the rainbows over the Falls were like the arts and beauty and goodness, with regard to the stream of life—caused by it, thrown upon its spray, but unable to stay or direct or affect it, and ceasing when it ceased. In all comparisons that rise in the heart, the river, with its multitudinous waves and its single current, likens itself to a life, whether of an individual or of a community. A man's life is of many flashing moments, and yet one stream; a nation's flows through all its citizens, and yet is more than they. In such places, one is aware, with an almost insupportable and yet comforting certitude, that both men and nations are hurried onwards to their ruin or ending as inevitably as this dark flood. Some go down to it unreluctant, and meet it, like the river, not without nobility. And as incessant, as inevitable, and as unavailing as the spray that hangs over the Falls, is the white cloud of human crying.... With some such thoughts does the platitudinous heart win from the confusion and thunder of Niagara a peace that the quietest plains or most stable hills can never give.

1. The Richelieu and Ontario Navigation Company steamer
Toronto, c. 1907. *Public Archives of Canada.*

*The great joy of travelling in Canada is to do it by water. The
advantage of this is that you can keep fairly clean and quiet of
nerves; the disadvantage is that you don't "see the country".*

From "Ontario".

2. King and Yonge Streets, Toronto, c. 1913. *City of Toronto Archives.*

*Toronto (pronounce T'ranto, please) is difficult to describe. It
has an individuality, but an elusive one; yet not through any
queerness or difficult shade of eccentricity; a subtly normal, an
indefinably obvious personality. It is a healthy, cheerful city (by
modern standards); a clean-shaven, pink-faced, respectably
dressed, fairly energetic, unintellectual, passably sociable, well-
to-do, public school-and-'varsity sort of city. . . .*

3. King Edward Hotel, c. 1919. *City of Toronto Archives.*

... But Toronto—Toronto is the subject. One must say something—what must one say about Toronto? What has anybody ever said? It is impossible to give it anything but commendation. It is not squalid like Birmingham, or cramped like Canton, or scattered like Edmonton, or sham like Berlin, or hellish like New York, or tiresome like Nice. It is all right. The only depressing thing is that it will always be what it is, only larger, and that no Canadian city can ever be anything better or different. If they are good they may become Toronto.

From "Ontario".

[69]

4. Arts and Letters Club, Toronto, 1916.

There's an Arts & Letters Club here, full of jolly people. I gave them a spare G.P. [Georgian Poetry]. They know of it, & they know our work. The leading newspaper interviewed me. Fame! Fame! A Canadian interview is a Solemn Thing.

From a letter to Harold Monro, en route to Winnipeg, 24 July 1913.

5. Toronto Islands, c. 1910. *Archives of Ontario.*

*Men have lived contentedly on this land and died
where they were born, and so given it a
certain sanctity.*

From "Ontario".

6. Rainham Township, Haldimand County, Ontario, 1906.
Archives of Ontario.

7. Niagara Falls from Clifton House, c. 1913. *City of Toronto Archives.*

The real secret of the beauty and terror of the Falls is not their height or width, but the feeling of colossal power and of unintelligible disaster caused by the plunge of that vast body of water. If that were taken away, there would be little visible change; but the heart would be gone.

From "Niagara Falls".

8. Aero cable car over whirlpool, Niagara Falls, c. 1916.
Public Archives of Canada.

III

BROOKE took the Grand Trunk railway west from Toronto to Sarnia and then boarded the steamer for the day-long trip north through Lake Huron to thriving Sault-Ste. Marie. He found the trip uncomfortable and lonely. It grew more so after they had squeezed through the Soo canal and left the cheery, populated shore to move out onto the broad expanse of Lake Superior. Brooke wrote to Edmund Gosse, the English literary scholar and poet:

> I'm writing on Lake Superior. We're steaming along in a little low fog, which just doesn't come up to the top deck, but completely hides the surface of the sea. Occasionally little cones and peaks of the mist float by, and the sun catches them. It is slightly uncanny, like everything in these great lakes. I have a perpetual feeling that a lake ought not to be this size. A river and a little lake and an ocean are natural; but not these creatures. They are too big, and too smooth, and too sunny; like an American business man.

He much preferred North American trains. At Port Arthur he boarded the C.P.R. for Winnipeg—a 400-mile journey through the Canadian shield which took more than twelve hours and cost him $12.90; his lower berth in the tourist car, which he favoured, was an extra $1.50.

Rupert had an introduction in Winnipeg to Howard Falk, an Old Rugbeian (known to his godfather, the Classics Master Robert Whitelaw). Falk and Brooke decided that they had

both had enough of cities and through an associate of Falk
secured an invitation to the Manitoba Fishing and Hunting
Club on Lake George, near Point du Bois, some seventy
rough miles northeast of Winnipeg. There Brooke spent his
twenty-sixth birthday, as he wrote to his mother, "with a gun
& fishing tackle & a canoe, without any clothes on, by a lake,
in a wood infested by bears, in a country where there aren't
ten people within five miles, & half of those are Indians".

He was more graphic in his letter to Cathleen Nesbitt:
"You'll excuse me if this letter is smeared with dirt or mud or
blood," he wrote. "I've all of them on my hands. The blood
may be mine or maybe a caribou's." He explained that he
and Falk were staying with Bryan, a veteran trapper, and his
wife, a recently-emigrated Liverpool scullery-maid who was
"just blossoming into a primitive in-touch-with-Nature squaw
woman". The trapper and "an Indian who lives near here"
had gone hunting one evening. Then:

> About 10.30 p.m., after our bonfire had died down, came a hail
> from the landing stage in the darkness below. The woman went
> out on to the rock we stand on to answer it, and came back
> with the news that 'the boys were to come down'. (It's very nice
> to be addressed 'Say, boys,—.') We went down the steep path, I
> ahead. By the boat-house in the darkness was Bryan (the
> trapper) wading ashore, tugging the canoe with two dark forms
> in it—the Indian, and, as I peered through the dark, something
> crouching with a vast head of horns. The woman said ''Ave ye
> shot anything?' Bryan replied 'Yaw. A rat.' (His form of
> humour.) The canoe came right up, and we distinguished an
> immense deer, the size of a small pony, dead, strapped into the
> bottom of the canoe. It weighed 500 lbs.: and they had paddled
> the canoe six miles, all round by the shore, the water up within
> half an inch of the gunwales, from the place where they'd shot
> him. They emptied him out into the muddy edge of the water;
> we lit a great fire of birch, spruce, and tamarack wood to see
> what was going on; and we all set to work to string him up for
> the night (he had been disembowelled.) For two hours we
> pulled and hauled at this creature, tugging at a rope over the
> branch of a birch. Then the trapper got an axe and hacked the
> beast's head off: with the great antlers it weighs some hundred
> pounds. At length we got the carcass hanging up and supported
> it with sticks. I got cut and scratched and smeared with the

creature's inside. It was a queer sight, lit up by the leaping flames of the fire, which the woman fed—the black water of the lake, muddy with trampling at the edge, and streaked with blood, the trapper in the tree, this great carcass hanging at one end of the rope, my friend and an Indian and I pulling our arms out at the other, the head gazing reproachfully at us from the ground, everybody using the most frightful language, and the rather ironical and very dispassionate stars above. Rather savage. Bryan said, once 'Brought it all the way home so as *you* could see it, kid', to his wife; so she was in an ecstasy of delight all evening.

Soon enough Brooke was on another shaky train journey heading across the prairies. By now he had more the measure of Canada, and his writing was showing a political tinge. He found the west, as he had hoped, more agreeable than eastern Canada. Winnipeggers, he thought, had "the free swing of Americans, without the bumptiousness", and they represented "a tempered democracy, a mitigated independence of bearing" that reflected his own temperament. As well, he had been exposed to the full force of Canadian regionalism; he referred now to the existence of several different Canadas, and well understood western grievances against eastern industrialists and bankers with their support of protective tariffs. He appreciated, too, that the niceties of the naval question meant little or nothing to the western farmer who wanted cheap machinery—wherever the source—cheaper freight rates, and unrestricted markets. All of Brooke's romantic notions of the boundless west, the brave Mounties, the dauntless pioneers, were taking flight, replaced by the realities of money-grubbing real-estate booms and endless statistics of growth—all presented tirelessly by fat-fisted promoters bulging with contrived statistics.

Brooke's Britishness continued to bob to the surface. He was most concerned about Canada's unbridled immigration, for he saw the scores of nationalities taking up land as "unassimilable lumps" which would weaken British blood. He didn't understand how people could live in such a bleak place although he did grant some merit to the windy beauty of a prairie landscape and sky.

He liked the honest civic pride he detected in western cities and he felt some of the new universities and public buildings showed determination, taste, and substance. Intellectual life was as scarce as it had been everywhere else in the "soulless Dominion" but he was delighted and amazed at the richness of the Calgary Public Library which he used as a barometer to gauge the cultural poverty elsewhere. The happiest sign he saw was the nascent co-operative movement among farmers. Brooke's old Fabianism rallied to this project as a way of the west remaining distinct, yet still contributing a moral and political force that might be felt throughout the country.

The newspapers too were saluting his political opinions. He wrote Eddie Marsh from Calgary:

> My progress is degenerating into a mere farce. The West insists on taking me seriously as a politician & thinker. Toronto... started in on me as a Poet with an Interview which I'll send you if I get a spare copy. It's only fairly funny, though it gets better when it's copied into *The Saskatoon Sentinel* & the rest, in fragments, as it does. Every little paper in Western Canada has started its Society Column with 'Dust' sometime in the last three weeks. Solemn thought. But in most of these towns they know me chiefly as a Political Expert. I average two reporters a day, who ask me my opinion on every subject under the sun. My opinions on the financial situation in Europe are good reading. And there are literally columns of them in the papers. I sit for an hour a day & laugh in my room. When I come back, though, I shall demand a knighthood from Winston. What's really wrong with these damned Canadians is that at bottom they all believe it's all play, & that war is impossible, & that there ain't no such place as the continent of Europe. They all live a thousand miles from the sea, and make an iniquitous living by gambling in real estate.

As usual he was more playful in his report (from Edmonton) to Cathleen Nesbitt:

> I find I'm becoming very thick-skinned and bold and the complete journalist. I've just been interviewed by a reporter. I fairly crushed him. I just put my cigar in the corner of my mouth, and undid my coat and put my thumbs under my arm pits, and spat, and said 'Say, kid, this is some town!' He asked me a lot of questions, of which I did not know the answer. So I

lied. I gave the poor old Westminster, for instance, a circula-
tion of a million, and a reputation that would make [editor]
Spender's few prim white hairs stand horrid to the heavens, if
he knew. Also, I am become very good at bearding people. I
just enter Railway offices, and demand free passes as a journalist. And I stamp into immense newspaper buildings and say 'I
want to talk for an hour to the Chief Editor'. And I can lean
across the counter with a cigarette and discuss the Heart with
the young lady who sells cigars, newspapers and stamps. I
believe I could do a deal in Real Estate in the bar over a John
Collins with a cleanshaven Yankee with a tremulous eyelid and
a moist lower-lip.

In fact, I am a Man.

TO WINNIPEG

THE boats that run from Sarnia the whole length of Lake Huron and Lake Superior are not comfortable. But no doubt a train for those six hundred miles would be worse. You start one afternoon, and in the morning of the next day you have done with the rather colourless, unindividual expanses of Huron, and are dawdling along a canal that joins the lakes by the little town of Sault-Ste. Marie (pronounced, abruptly, "Soo"). We happened on it one Sunday. The nearer waters of the river and the lakes were covered with little sailing or rowing or bathing parties. Everybody seemed cheerful, merry, and mildly raucous. There is a fine, breezy, enviable healthiness about Canadian life. Except in some Eastern cities, there are few clerks or working-men but can get away to the woods and water.

As we drew out into the cold magnificence of Lake Superior, the receding woody shores were occasionally spotted with picnickers or campers, who rushed down the beach in various *déshabillé*, waving towels, handkerchiefs, or garments. We were as friendly. The human race seemed a jolly bunch, and the world a fine, pleasant, open-air affair—"some world", in fact. A man in a red shirt and a bronzed girl with flowing hair slid past in a canoe. We whistled, sang, and cried "Snooky-ook-ums!" and other words of occult meaning, which imputed love to them, and foolishness. They replied suitably, grinned, and were gone. A little old lady in black, in the chair next mine, kept a small telescope glued to her eye, hour after hour. Whenever she distinguished life on any shore we passed, she waved a tiny handkerchief. Diligently she did this, and with grave face, never visible to the objects of her devotion, I suppose, but certainly very happy; the most persistent lover of humanity I have ever seen.

In the afternoon we were beyond sight of land. The world grew a little chilly; and over the opaque, hueless water came sliding a queer, pale mist. We strained through it for hours, a low bank of cloud, not twenty feet in height, on which one could look down from the higher deck. Its upper surface was quite flat and smooth, save for innumerable tiny molehills or pyramids of mist. We seemed to be ploughing aimlessly through the phantasmal sand-dunes of another world, faintly and by an accident apprehended. So may the shades on a ghostly liner, plunging down Lethe, have an hour's chance glimpse of the lights and lives of Piccadilly, to them uncertain and filmy mirages of the air.

To taste the full deliciousness of travelling in an American train by night through new scenery, you must carefully secure a lower berth. And when you are secret and separate in your little oblong world, safe between sheets, pull up the blinds on the great window a few inches and leave them so. Thus, as you lie, you can view the dark procession of woods and hills, and mingle the broken hours of railway slumber with glimpses of a wild starlit landscape. The country retains individuality, and yet puts on romance, especially the rough, shaggy region between Port Arthur and Winnipeg. For four hundred miles there is hardly a sign that humanity exists on the earth's face, only rocks and endless woods of scrubby pine, and the occasional strange gleam of water, and

night and the wind. Night-long, dream and reality mingle. You may wake from sleep to find yourself flying
through a region where a forest fire has passed, a place
of grey pine-trunks, stripped of foliage, occasionally waving a naked bough. They appear stricken by calamity,
intolerably bare and lonely, gaunt, perpetually protest-
ing, amazed and tragic creatures. We saw no actual fire
the night I passed. But a little while after dawn we
noticed on the horizon, fifteen miles away, an immense
column of smoke. There was little wind, and it hung, as
if sculptured, against the grey of the morning; nor did
we lose sight of it till just before we boomed over a
wide, swift, muddy river, into the flat city of Winnipeg.

Winnipeg is the West. It is important and obvious that
in Canada there are two or three (some say five) distinct
Canadas. Even if you lump the French and English
together as one community in the East, there remains
the gulf of the Great Lakes. The difference between
East and West is possibly no greater than that between
North and South England, or Bavaria and Prussia; but
in this country, yet unconscious of itself, there is so
much less to hold them together. The character of the
land and the people differs; their interests, as it appears
to them, are not the same. Winnipeg is a new city. In
the archives at Ottawa is a picture of Winnipeg in 1870
—Mainstreet, with a few shacks, and the prairie either
end. Now her population is a hundred thousand, and
she has the biggest this, that, and the other west of
Toronto. A new city; a little more American than the
other Canadian cities, but not unpleasantly so. The
streets are wider, and full of a bustle which keeps clear
of hustle. The people have something of the free swing
of Americans, without the bumptiousness; a tempered
democracy, a mitigated independence of bearing. The
manners of Winnipeg, of the West, impress the stranger
as better than those of the East, more friendly, more
hearty, more certain to achieve graciousness, if not
grace. There is, even, in the architecture of Winnipeg, a

sort of gauche pride visible. It is hideous, of course, even
more hideous than Toronto or Montreal; but cheerily
and windily so. There is no scheme in the city, and no
beauty, but it is at least preferable to Birmingham, less
dingy, less directly depressing. It has no real slums, even
though there is poverty and destitution.

But there seems to be a trifle more public spirit in the
West than the East. Perhaps it is that in the greater
eagerness and confidence of this newer country men
have a superfluity of energy and interest, even after
attending to their own affairs, to give to the community.
Perhaps it is that the West is so young that one has a
suspicion money-making has still some element of a
child's game in it—its only excuse. At any rate, whether
because the state of affairs is yet unsettled, or because of
the invisible subtle spirit of optimism that blows through
the heavily clustering telephone-wires and past the neat
little modern villas and down the solidly pretentious
streets, one can't help finding a tiny hope that Winnipeg, the city of buildings and the city of human beings,
may yet come to something. It is a slender hope, not to
be compared to that of the true Winnipeg man, who,
gazing on his city, is fired with the proud and secret
ambition that it will soon be twice as big, and after that
four times, and then ten times. . . .

> Wider still and wider
> Shall thy bounds be set,

says that hymn which is the noblest expression of modern ambition. *That* hope is sure to be fulfilled. But the
other timid prayer, that something different, something
more worth having, may come out of Winnipeg, exists,
and not quite unreasonably. That cannot be said of
Toronto.

Winnipeg is of the West, new, vigorous in its way, of
unknown potentialities. Already the West has been a
nuisance to the East, in the fight of 1911 over Reciproc-

ity with the United States. When she gets a larger representation in Parliament, she will be still more of a nuisance. A casual traveller cannot venture to investigate the beliefs and opinions of the inhabitants of a country, but he can record them all the better, perhaps, for his foreign-ness. It is generally believed in the West that the East runs Canada, and runs it for its own advantage. And the East means a very few rich men, who control the big railways, the banks, and the Manufacturers' Association, subscribe to both political parties, and are generally credited with complete control over the Tariff and most other Canadian affairs. Whether or not the Manufacturers' Association does arrange the Tariff and control the commerce of Canada, it is generally believed to do so. The only thing is that its friends say that it acts in the best interests of Canada, its enemies that it acts in the best interests of the Manufacturers' Association. Among its enemies are many in the West. The normal Western life is a lonely and individual one; and a large part of the population has crossed from the United States, or belongs to that great mass of European immigration that Canada is letting so blindly in. So, naturally, the Westerner does not feel the same affection for the Empire or for England as the British Canadians of the East, whose forefathers fought to stay within the Empire. Nor is his affection increased by the suspicion that the Imperial cry has been used for party purposes. He has no use for politics at Ottawa. The naval question is nothing to him. He wants neither to subscribe money nor to build ships. Europe is very far away; and he is too ignorant to realise his close connection with her. He has strong views, however, on a Tariff which only affects him by perpetually raising the cost of living and farming. The ideas of even a Conservative in the West about reducing the Tariff would make an Eastern "Liberal" die of heart-failure. And the Westerner also hates the Banks. The banking system of Canada is peculiar, and throws the control of the banks into the hands of a few people in the East, who were felt, by the ever optimistic West, to have shut down credit too completely during the recent money stringency.

The most interesting expression of the new Western point of view, and in many ways the most hopeful movement in Canada, is the Co-operative movement among the graingrowers of the three prairie provinces. Only started a few years ago, it has grown rapidly in numbers, wealth, power, and extent of operations. So far it has confined itself politically to influencing provincial legislatures. But it has gradually attached itself to an advanced Radical programme of a Chartist description. And it is becoming powerful. Whether the outcome will be a very desirable rejuvenation of the Liberal Party, or the creation of a third—perhaps Radical-Labour—party, it is hard to tell. At any rate, the change will come. And, just to start with, there will very shortly come to the Eastern Powers, who threw out Reciprocity with the States for the sake of the Empire, a demand from the West that the preference to British goods be increased rapidly till they be allowed to come in free, also for the Empire's sake. Then the fun will begin.

OUTSIDE

I HAD visited New York, Boston, Quebec, Montreal, and Toronto. In Winnipeg I found a friend, who was tired of cities. So was I. In Canada the remedy lies close at hand. We took ancient clothes—and I, Ben Jonson and Jane Austen to keep me English—and departed northward for a lodge, reported to exist in a region of lakes and hills and forests and caribou and Indians and a few people. At first the train sauntered through a smiling plain, intermittently cultivated, and dotted with little new villages. Over this country are thrown little pools of that flood of European immigration that pours through Winnipeg, to remain separate or be absorbed, as destiny wills. The problem of immigration here reveals that purposelessness that exists in the affairs of Canada even more than those of other nations. The multitude from South of East Europe flocks in. Some make money and return. The most remain, often in inassimilable lumps. There is every sign that these lumps may poison the health of Canada as dangerously as they have that of the United States. For Canada there is the peril of too large an element of foreign blood and traditions in a small nation already little more than half composed of British blood and descent. Nationalities seem to teach one another only their worst. If the Italians gave the Canadians of their good manners, and the Doukhobors or Poles inoculated them with idealism and the love of beauty, and received from them British romanticism and sense of responsibility! ... But they only seem to increase the anarchy, these "foreigners", and to learn the American twang and method of spitting. And there is the peril of politics. Upon these scattered exotic communities, ignorant of the problems of their adopted land, ignorant even of its language, swoop the agents of political parties, with their one effectual argument—bad whisky. This baptism is the immigrants' only organised welcome into their new liberties. Occasionally some Church raises a thin protest. But the "Anglo-Saxon" continues to take up his burden; and the floods from Europe pour in. Canadians regard this influx with that queer fatalism which men adopt under plutocracy. "How could they stop it? It pays the steamship and railway companies. It may, or may not, be good for Canada. Who knows? In any case, it will go on. Our masters wish it. . . . "

It is noteworthy that Icelanders are found to be far the readiest to mingle and become Canadian. After them, Norwegians and Swedes. With other immigrant nationalities, hope lies with the younger generation; but these acclimatise immediately.

Our train was boarded by a crowd of Ruthenians or Galicians, brown-eyed and beautiful people, not yet wholly civilised out of their own costume. The girls chatted together in a swift, lovely language, and the children danced about, tossing their queer brown mops of hair. They clattered out at a little village that seemed to belong to them. I pondered on their feelings, and looked for the name of the little Utopia these aliens had found in a new world. It was called (for the railway companies name towns in this country) "Milner".

We wandered into rougher country, where the rocks begin to show through the surface, and scrub pine abounds. At the end of our side-line was another, and at the end of that a village, the ultimate outpost of civilisation. Here, on the way back, some weeks later, we had to spend the night in a little hotel which "accommodated transients". It was a rough affair of planks, inhabited by whatever wandering workman from construction-camps or other labour in the region wanted shelter for the night. You slept in a sort of dormitory, each bed partitioned off from the rest by walls that were some feet short of the ceiling. Swedes, Germans, Welsh, Italians, and Poles occupied the other partitions, each blaspheming the works of the Lord in his own tongue. About midnight two pairs of feet crashed into the cell opposite mine; and a high, sleepless voice, with an accent I knew, continued an interminable argument on theology. "I' beginning wash word," it proclaimed with all the melancholy of drunkenness. The other disputant was German or Norwegian, and uninterested, though very kindly. "Right-o!" he said. "Let's go sleep!"

"What word?" pondered the Englishman. The Norwegian suggested several, sleepily. "Logos," wailed the other, "*What* Logos?" and wept. They persisted, hour by hour, disconnected voices in the void and darkness, lonely and chance companions in the back-blocks of Canada, the one who couldn't and the one who didn't want to, understand. A little before dawn I woke again. That thin voice, in patient soliloquy, was discussing Female Suffrage, going very far down into the roots of the matter. I met its owner next morning. He was tall and dark and lachrymose, with bloodshot eyes, and breath that stank of gin. He had played scrum-half for —— College in '98; and had prepared for ordination. "You'll understand, old man," he said, "how out of place I am amongst this scum—οἱ πολλοί—we're not of the οἱ πολλοί are we?" It seemed nicer to agree. "Oh, I know Greek!" —he was too eagerly the gentleman— " ὁ κόσμος τῆς ἀδικίας—the last thing I learnt for ordination—this world of injustice—that's right, isn't it?" He

laughed sickly. "I say, as one 'Varsity man to another—
we're not οἱ πολλοί—could you lend me some money?"

We had to press on thirty miles up a "light railway"
to a power-station, a settlement by a waterfall in the
wild. An engine and an ancient luggage-van conveyed
us. The van held us, three crates, and some sacks, four
half-breeds in black slouch hats, who curled up on the
floor like dogs and slept, and an aged Italian. This last
knew no word of English. He had travelled all the way
from Naples, Heaven knows how, to find his two sons,
supposed to be working in the power-station. So much
was written on a piece of paper. We gave him chocolate,
and at intervals I repeated to him my only Italian, the
first line of the *Divina Commedia*. He seemed cheered.
The van jolted on through the fading light. Once a man
stepped out on to the track, stopped us, and clambered
silently up. We went on. It was the doctor, who had
been visiting some lonely hut in the woods. Later,
another figure was seen staggering between the rails. We
slowed up, shouted, and finally stopped, butting him
gently on the back with our buffers, and causing him to
fall. He was very drunk. The driver and the doctor
helped him into the van. There he stood, and looking
round, said very distinctly, "I do not wish to travel on
your —— train." So we put him off again, and proceeded. Such is the West.

We rattled interminably through the darkness. The
unpeopled woods closed about us, snatched with lean
branches, and opened out again to a windy space. Once
or twice the ground fell away, and there was, for a
moment, the mysterious gleam and stir of water. Canadian stars are remote and virginal. Everyone slumbered.
Arrival at the great concrete building and the little
shacks of the power-station shook us to our feet. The
Italian vanished into the darkness. Whether he found his
sons or fell into the river no one knew, and no one
seemed to care.

An Indian, taciturn and Mongolian, led us on next

day, by boat and on foot, to the lonely log-house we aimed at. It stood on high rocks, above a lake six miles by two. There was an Indian somewhere, by a river three miles west, and a trapper to the east, and a family encamped on an island in the lake. Else nobody.

It is that feeling of fresh loneliness that impresses itself before any detail of the wild. The soul—or the personality—seems to have indefinite room to expand. There is no one else within reach, there never has been anyone; no one else is *thinking* of the lakes and hills you see before you. They have no tradition, no names even; they are only pools of water and lumps of earth, some day, perhaps, to be clothed with loves and memories and the comings and goings of men, but now dumbly waiting their Wordsworth or their Acropolis to give them individuality, and a soul. In such country as this there is a rarefied clean sweetness. The air is unbreathed, and the earth untrodden. All things share this childlike loveliness, the grey whispering reeds, fir-trees that make up these forests, even the brisk touch of the clear water as you dive.

That last sensation, indeed, and none of sight or hearing, has impressed itself as the token of Canada, the land. Every swimmer knows it. It is not languorous, like bathing in a warm Southern sea; nor grateful, like a river in a hot climate; nor strange, as the ocean always is; nor startling, like very cold water. But it touches the body continually with freshness, and it seems to be charged with a subtle and unexhausted energy. It is colourless, faintly stinging, hard and grey, like the rocks around, full of vitality, and sweet. It has the tint and sensation of a pale dawn before the sun is up. Such is the wild of Canada. It awaits the sun, the end for which Heaven made it, the blessing of civilisation. Some day it will be sold in large portions, and the timber given to a friend of ——'s, and cut down and made into paper, on which shall be printed the praise of prosperity; and the land itself shall be divided into town-lots and sold, and sub-divided and sold again, and boomed and resold, and boosted and distributed to fishy young men who will vend it in distant parts of the country; and then such portions as can never be built upon shall be given in exchange for great sums of money to old ladies in the quieter parts of England, but the central parts of towns shall remain in the hands of the wise. And on these shall churches, hotels, and a great many ugly skyscrapers be built, and hovels for the poor, and houses for the rich, none beautiful, and there shall ugly objects be manufactured, rather hurriedly, and sold to the people at more than they are worth, because similar and cheaper objects made in other countries are kept out by a tariff.

But at present there are only the wrinkled, grey-blue lake, sliding ever sideways, and the grey rocks, and the cliffs and hills, covered with birch-trees, and the fresh wind among the birches, and quiet, and that unseizable virginity. Dawn is always a lost pearly glow in the ashen skies, and sunset a multitude of softly-tinted mists sliding before a remotely golden West. They follow one another with an infinite loneliness. And there is a far and solitary beach of dark, golden sand, close by a deserted Indian camp, where, if you drift quietly round the corner in a canoe, you may see a bear stumbling along, or a great caribou, or a little red deer coming down to the water to drink, treading the wild edge of lake and forest with a light, secret, and melancholy grace.

THE PRAIRIES

I PASSED the last few hours of the westward journey from Winnipeg to Regina in daylight, the daylight of a wet and cheerless Sunday. The car was half-empty, in possession of a family of small children and some theatrical ladies and gentlemen from the United States, travelling on "one night stands", who were collectively called "The World-Renowned Barbary Pirates". We jogged limply from little village to little village, each composed of little brown log-shacks, with a few buildings of tin and corrugated iron, and even of brick, and several grain-elevators. Each village—I beg your pardon, "town"—seems to be exactly like the next. They differ a little in size, from populations of a hundred to nearly two thousand, and in age, for some have buildings dating almost back to the nineteenth century, and a few are still mostly tents. They seemed all to be emptied of their folk this Sabbath morn; though whether the inhabitants were at work, or in church, or had shot themselves from depression induced by the weather, it was impossible to tell. These little towns do not look to the passer-by comfortable as homes. Partly, there is the difficulty of distinguishing your village from the others. It would be as bad as being married to a Jap. And then towns should be on hills or in valleys, however small. A town dumped down, apparently by chance, on a flat expanse, wears the same air of discomfort as a man trying to make his bed on a level, unyielding surface such as a lawn or pavement. He feels hopelessly incidental to the superficies of the earth. He is aware that the human race has thigh-bones.

Yet this country is not quite flat, as I had been led to expect. It does not give you that feeling of a plain you have in parts of Lombardy and Holland and Belgium. This may have been due to the grey mist and drizzle which curtained off the horizon. But the land was always very slightly rolling, and sometimes almost as uneven as a Surrey common. At first it seemed to be given to mixed farming a good deal; afterwards to wheat, oats, and barley. But a great part is uncultivated prairie-land, grass, with sparse bushes and patches of brushwood and a few rare trees, and continual clumps of large golden daisies. Occasional rough black roads wind through the brush and into the towns, and die into grass tracks along the wire fences. The day I went through, the interminable, oblique, thin rain took the gold out of the wheat and the brown from the distant fields and bushes, and drabbed all the colours in the grass. The children in the car cried to each other with the shrill, sick persistency of tired childhood, "How many inches to Regina?" "A Billion." "A Trillion." "A Shillion." The Barbary Pirates laughed incessantly. It seemed to me that the prairie would be a lonely place to live in, especially if it rained. But the people who have lived there for years tell me they get very homesick if they go away for a time. Valleys and hills seem to them petty, fretful, unlovable. The magic of the plains has them in thrall.

Certainly there is a little more democracy in the west of Canada than the east; the communities seem a little less incapable of looking after themselves. Out in the west they are erecting not despicable public buildings, founding universities, running a few public services.

That "politics" has a voice in these undertakings does
not make them valueless. There are perceptible in the
prairies, among all the corruption, irresponsibility, and
disastrous individualism, some faint signs of the sense of
the community. Take a very good test, the public libraries. As you traverse Canada from east to west they
steadily improve. You begin in the city of Montreal,
which is unable to support one, and pass through the
dingy rooms and inadequate intellectual provision of
Toronto and Winnipeg. After that the libraries and read-
ing-rooms, small for the smaller cities, are cleaner and
better kept, show signs of care and intelligence; until at
last, in Calgary, you find a very neat and carefully kept
building, stocked with an immense variety of periodicals,
and an admirably chosen store of books, ranging from
the classics to the most utterly modern literature. Few
large English towns could show anything as good. Cross
the Rockies to Vancouver, and you're back among dirty
walls, grubby furniture, and inadequate literature again.
There's nothing in Canada to compare with the magnifi-
cent libraries little New Zealand can show. But Calgary
is hopeful.

These cities grow in population with unimaginable
velocity. From thirty to thirty thousand in fifteen years
is the usual rate. Pavements are laid down, stores and
bigger stores and still bigger stores spring up. Trams
buzz along the streets towards the unregarded horizon
that lies across the end of most roads in these flat,
geometrically planned, prairie-towns. Probably a
Chinese quarter appears, and the beginnings of slums.
Expensive and pleasant small dwelling-houses fringe the
outskirts; and rents being so high, great edifices of residential flats rival the great stores. In other streets, or
even sandwiched between the finer buildings, are dingy
and decaying saloons, and innumerable little booths and
hovels where adventurers deal dishonestly in Real
Estate, and Employment Bureaux. And there are the
vast erections of the great corporations, Hudson's Bay

Company, and the banks and the railways, and, sometimes almost equally impressive, the public buildings.
There are the beginnings of very costly Universities; and
Regina has built a superb great House of Parliament,
with a wide sheet of water in front of it, a noble building.

The inhabitants of these cities are proud of them, and
envious of each other with a bitter rivalry. They do not
love their cities as a Manchester man loves Manchester
or a Münchener Munich, for they have probably lately
arrived in them, and will surely pass on soon. But while
they are there they love them, and with no silent love.
They boost. To boost is to commend outrageously. And
each cries up his own city, both from pride, it would
appear, and for profit. For the fortunes of Newville are
very really the fortunes of its inhabitants. From the
successful speculator, owner of whole blocks, to the
waiter bringing you a Martini, who has paid up a frac-
tion of the cost of a quarter-share in a town-lot—all are
the richer, as well as the prouder, if Newville grows. It is
imperative to praise Edmonton in Edmonton. But it is
sudden death to praise it in Calgary. The partisans of
each city proclaim its superiority to all the others in
swiftness of growth, future population, size of buildings,
price of land—by all recognised standards of excellence.
I travelled from Edmonton to Calgary in the company
of a citizen of Edmonton and a citizen of Calgary. Hour
after hour they disputed. Land in Calgary had risen
from five dollars to three hundred; but in Edmonton
from three to five hundred. Edmonton had grown from
thirty persons to forty thousand in twenty years; but
Calgary from twenty to thirty thousand in twelve. . . .
"Where"—as a respite—"did I come from?" I had to tell
them, not without shame, that my own town of Grantchester, having numbered three hundred at the time of
Julius Caesar's landing, had risen rapidly to nearly four
by Doomsday Book, but was now declined to three-fifty.
They seemed perplexed and angry.

Sentimental people in the East will talk of the romance of the West, and of these simple, brave pioneers who have wrung a living from the soil, and are properly proud of the rude little towns that mark their conquest over nature. That may apply to the frontiers of civilisation up North, but the prairie-towns have progressed beyond all that. A few of the old pioneers of the West survive to watch with startled eyes the wonderful fruits of the seed they sowed. Such are among the finest people in Canada, very different from the younger generation, with wider interests, good talkers, the best of company. From them, and from records, one can learn of the early settlers and the beginnings of the North-West Mounted Police. The Police seem to have been superb. For no great reward, but the love of the thing, they imposed order and fairness upon half a continent. The Indians trusted them utterly; they were without fear. A store stands now in Calgary where forty years ago a policeman was shot to death by a murderer, followed over a thousand miles. He knew that the criminal would shoot; but it was the rule of the Mounted Police not to fire first. Wounded, he killed his man, then died. And there was the case of the desperado who crossed the border, and was eventually captured and held by an immense force of American police and military. They awaited a regiment of the Police to conduct the villain back to trial. Two appeared, and being asked, "Where is the escort?" replied, "We are the escort," and started back their five hundred miles ride with the murderer in tow. And there were the two who pursued a horse-thief from Dawson down to Minneapolis, caught him, and took him back to Dawson to be hanged. And there was the settler, who. . . .

The tragedy of the West is that these men have passed, and that what they lived and died to secure for their race is now the foundation for a gigantic national gambling of a most unprofitable and disastrous kind. Hordes of people—who mostly seem to come from the

great neighbouring Commonwealth, and are inspired
with the national hunger for getting rich quickly without
deserving it—prey on the community by their dealings in
what is humorously called "Real Estate". For them our
fathers died. What a sowing, and what a harvest! And
where good men worked or perished is now a row of
little shops, all devoted to the sale of town-lots in some
distant spot that must infallibly become a great city in
the next two years, and in the doorway of each lounges
a thin-chested, much-spitting youth, with a flabby face,
shifty eyes, and an inhuman mouth, who invites you
continually, with the most raucous of American accents,
to "step inside and ex-amine our Praposition".

1. Winnipeg. *Library of King's College, Cambridge.*

Winnipeg is a new city. In the archives at Ottawa is a picture of Winnipeg in 1870—Mainstreet, with a few shacks, and the prairie either end. Now her population is a hundred thousand, and she has the biggest this, that, and the other west of Toronto.

From "To Winnipeg".

2. Galician settlers, Stuartburn, Manitoba, n.d.

Public Archives of Canada.

Over this country are thrown little pools of that flood of European immigration that pours through Winnipeg, to remain separate or be absorbed, as destiny wills.

From "Outside".

3.   Two canoes, with hunters, dogs and deer. n.d. *Public Archives of Canada.*

*The trapper and an Indian killed a caribou buck two evenings
ago, a sort of stag, the size of a small pony, & brought it back &
we spent the night from 10-12:30 in trying to hang it up on a
tree by the boathouse, to keep it clear of the ground for the
night. The man cut its head off, & skinned it next morning, &
we have been living on the meat since—very good it is. It was a
queer scene that night, we three & the Indian trying to hoist this
immense brute up, with its fine antlers, all by the light of a great
bonfire we had lit for the purpose. But don't tell any Canadians
about it. If the authorities knew the Trapper would get fined 50
dollars, as it's out of season for caribou.*

From a letter to his mother, Lake George, Manitoba, 3 August 1913.

4. Parliament Buildings, Regina, Saskatchewan, 1913.

Public Archives of Canada.

*And there are the vast erections of the great corporations,
Hudson's Bay Company, and the banks and the railways, and,
sometimes almost equally impressive, the public buildings. There
are the beginnings of very costly Universities; and Regina has
built a superb great House of Parliament, with a wide sheet of
water in front of it, a noble building.*

From "The Prairies".

5.   Yorkton, Saskatchewan, n.d. *Archives of Ontario.*

*We jogged limply from little village to little village, each
composed of little brown log-shacks, with a few buildings of tin
and corrugated iron, and even of brick, and several grain-
elevators. Each village—I beg your pardon, "town"—seems to be
exactly like the next. They differ a little in size, from
populations of a hundred to nearly two thousand, and in age, for
some have buildings dating almost back to the nineteenth
century, and a few are still mostly tents.*

From "The Prairies".

6. Public Library, Calgary, Alberta, n.d. *Public Archives of Canada.*

At last, in Calgary, you find a very neat and carefully kept building, stocked with an immense variety of periodicals, and an admirably chosen store of books, ranging from the classics to the most utterly modern literature. Few large English towns could show anything as good.

From "The Prairies".

7. Cowboy, Prairies, c. 1909. *Archives of Ontario.*

8.   Immigrant school children, near Lamont, Alberta, 1909.
Archives of Ontario.

You can't think how sick one's heart gets for something old.
For weeks I have not seen or touched a town so old as myself.
Horrible! Horrible! They gather round me & say, "In 1901
Calgary had 139 inhabitants, now it has 75,000" & so forth. I
reply, "My village is also growing. At the time of Julius Caesar
it was a bare 300. Domesday Book gave it 347 and it is now
close on 390." Which is ill-mannered of me.

Letter to Edward Marsh, Calgary, 16 August [1913].

9. Postman, Edmonton, Alberta, c. 1909. *Archives of Ontario.*

RUPERT Brooke had the common European fantasy about North American Indians based on the "Red Indians" of the Boy's Own adventure stories of his youth. Like Archie Belaney, the Englishman who later conned the world as Grey Owl, Rupert had a fascination and an empathy for what he thought was the simple natural life of the "noble savage".

In Ottawa Duncan Campbell Scott had disabused him of much of this romantic notion, but Brooke retained an attitude to the Indians which, while sympathetic, smacked of paternalism. Brooke eagerly accepted Scott's letters of introduction to various Indian agents in the west, and encouraged by his Toronto friend Edmund Morris's talk about the Stoney tribe, paid a visit to their reservation near Calgary. He was both moved and saddened by the experience. "What will happen?" he asked:

> Shall we preserve these few bands of them, untouched, to succeed us, ultimately, when the grasp of our 'civilisation' weakens, and our transient anarchy in these wilder lands recedes once more before the older anarchy of Nature? Or will they be entirely swallowed by that ugliness of shops and trousers with which we enchain the earth, and become a memory and less than a memory?

Brooke was right to be concerned. By 1913 the Indian population of Canada was just over 100,000. Indian tribes,

emasculated by the loss of their traditional means of livelihood and most of their culture, were reduced to a kind of
government charity on the reserves. And they were still rav-
aged by the white man's devastating diseases, especially
tuberculosis and smallpox. Brooke felt the government's
efforts were "well-intentioned" but had effaced the emotional
dignity of the Indian; he admitted that the Indian needed
protection from whites and that the reserves gave some measure of this, but he couldn't see to what end. Was the Indian
to be assimilated, or to become a museum piece? He concluded that half-breeds were the most unfortunate victims for
"most appear to inherit the weaknesses of both sides".

Brooke's analysis of the Indian is unique in his writing
about North America. For the first time he looks less at
Canadian or American civilization as opposed to the influence of Western civilization as a whole. The tragedy of the
Indians, for him, was the fault of all Western societies and
brought sharply into question the moral basis of European
culture. He would have similar reflections in the South Seas.

But Brooke could never be entirely serious, at least not for
long, and he wrote Cathleen Nesbitt a theatrical presentation
of his visit to the Stonies which he knew she would enjoy:

> Oh, but the Indians. They were so fine looking, and so jolly.
> They kept coming into the store-office to ask for things—the
> agents are father mother aunt priest doctor lawyer M.P. house-
> maid and God to the Indians in their charge. An Indian in a
> blanket and fur and gaudy trimmings would sidle into the
> room. Then for ten minutes he would stand silent. You must
> never hurry an Indian. Then he takes the pipe out of his
> mouth, says 'Um' and puts it back again. Five minutes pass.
> Then he looks at the ceiling, and says: '...Um...Salt. Um.'
> The Agent. 'Is it more Epsom's Fruit Salts y'r wanting?'
> Indian (nods).
> Agent. 'But ye had som th'ither day—'
> Indian (blank).
> Agent. 'Is y'r stomach onaisy?'
> Indian (nods).
> Agent (getting up, taking jar, pouring out some salts into
> paper, and wrapping them up). 'There you are.'
> Indian (secretes them in some pouch, without a word).

Agent sits down again.
Indian stands for ten minutes silent and immobile.
Indian (suddenly) ' ... Um ... '
Exit slowly.
Enter 2nd Indian, cautiously.
  (da capo)
But they're far nicer than the other inhabitants of this conti-
nent.

By 25 August Rupert was in the Rockies (more precisely
the Selkirks) and here felt "beauty ... for the first time in
Canada, the real beauty that is always too sudden for mortal
eyes, and brings pain with its comfort". Banff, "an ordinary
little tourist-resort", didn't interest him very much. It was
"beautiful enough, and invigorating. But Lake Louise—Lake
Louise is of another world."

He stayed at the Chateau for several days, wrote a postcard to his mother and a short note to Cathleen, and then
simply relaxed—"not a line or a word of prose or verse has
flowed from my pen. I am just one of the idle rich. Tra! la!"
Brooke's time in the mountains was his happiest in Canada.
He told his mother that he was "enjoying himself
immensely". Cathleen was pitied for "sweating away in a hot
and stupid London" while he passed the time "lounging and
staring at the lake and the mountains and the snow. It is the
most beautiful place in the world. Just sheer beauty. So I eat
and chatter and roam and look."

Brooke had actually done a little more than that. The
intermittent bouts of bouyancy and depression which had
followed him from England subsided at least in part because
at Lake Louise he met a woman: the widow Marchesa
Capponi (like so many minor and major noblewomen of the
late nineteenth and early twentieth centuries—an American).
Brooke was now in good form—physically, mentally and
emotionally. By the time he reached the Rockies some of his
ultra-Englishness had drained from him. He was now seeing
Canada more for what it was and avoiding simple comparisons. That's not to say that he liked what he saw, but with
the Rockies his understanding seems clear and uncluttered.

One thing is certain—he liked the Marchesa Capponi. He wrote to her from Vancouver:

I was lonely after you'd gone. I turned straight and climbed to Lake Agnes, and there sat and looked at the valley down which your train had vanished. After a bit seven females rushed up and said 'We have seen a bear. Will you protect us back to the Hotel S?' I replied 'I want to be alone. There are already too many females in the world. Go. And I hope you meet the bear.' They went. And I could not see them in the hotel that evening. I suppose they did meet the Bear.... I was afflicted by inspiration all yesterday in the train. Sehr peinlich. For I had ideas for seven poems and was too tired to write any. Now, I am waiting for my big luggage to appear. When it does, I shall have a bath, and change. I pass the odd few minutes in writing thus dully to you. There are only two chairs in my room. I am sitting on one. I wish you were sitting on the other.... At Field an Eastward train came in, labelled—Minneapolis and St. Paul.... When no one was looking I stole behind and affixed a tiny kiss to the rear buffer. Did it get to you? I feared it might fall off.

THE INDIANS

WHEN I was in the East, I got to know a man who had spent many years of his life living among the Indians. He showed me his photographs. He explained one, of an old woman. He said, "They told me there was an old woman in the camp called Laughing Earth. When I heard the name, I just said, 'Take me to her!' She wouldn't be photographed. She kept turning her back to me. I just picked up a clod and plugged it at her, and said, 'Turn round, Laughing Earth!' She turned half round, and grinned. She *was* a game old bird! I joshed all the boys here Laughing Earth was my girl— till they saw her photo!"

There stands Laughing Earth, in brightly-coloured petticoat and blouse, her grey hair blowing about her. Her back is towards you, but her face is turned, and scarcely hidden by a hand that is raised with all the coyness of seventy years. Laughter shines from the infinitely lined, round, brown cheeks, and from the mouth, and from the dancing eyes, and floods and spills over from each of the innumerable wrinkles. Laughing Earth —there is endless vitality in that laughter. The hand and face and the old body laugh. No skinny, intellectual mirth, affecting but the lips! It was the merriment of an apple bobbing on the bough, or a brown stream running over rocks, or any other gay creature of earth. And with all was a great dignity, invulnerable to clods, and a kindly and noble beauty. By the light of that laughter much becomes clear—the right place of man upon earth, the entire suitability in life of very brightly-coloured petticoats, and the fact that old age is only a different kind of a merriment from youth, and a wiser.

And by that light the fragments of this pathetic race become more comprehensible, and, perhaps, less pathetic. The wanderer in Canada sees them from time to time, the more the further west he goes, irrelevant and inscrutable figures. In the East, French and Scotch half-breeds frequent the borders of civilisation. In any Western town you may chance on a brave and his wife and a baby, resplendent in gay blankets and trappings, sliding gravely through the hideousness of the new order that has supplanted them. And there will be a few half-breeds loitering at the corners of the streets. These people of mixed race generally seem unfortunate in the first generation. A few of the older ones, the "old-timers", have "made good", and hold positions in the society for which they pioneered. But most appear to inherit the weaknesses of both sides. Drink does its work. And the nobler ones, like the tragic figure of that poetess who died recently, Pauline Johnson, seem fated to be at odds with the world. The happiest, whether Indian or half-breed, are those who live beyond the ever-advancing edges of cultivation and order, and force a livelihood from nature by hunting and fishing. Go anywhere into the wild, and you will find in little clearings, by lake or river, a dilapidated hut with a family of these solitaries, friendly with the pioneers or trappers around, ready to act as guide on hunt or trail. The Government, extraordinarily painstaking and well-intentioned, has established Indian schools, and trains some of them to take their places in the civilisation we have built. Not the best Indians these, say lovers of the race. I have met them, as clerks or stenographers, only distinguishable from their neighbours by a darker skin and a sweeter voice and manner. And in a generation or two, I suppose, the strain mingles and is lost. So we finish with kindness what our fathers began with war.

The Government, and others, have scientifically studied the history and characteristics of the Indians, and written them down in books, lest it be forgotten that human beings could be so extraordinary. They were a wandering race, it appears, of many tribes and, even, languages. Not apt to arts or crafts, they had, and have, an unrefined delight in bright colours. They enjoyed a "Nature-Worship", believed rather dimly in a presiding Power, and very definitely in certain ethical and moral rules. One of their incomprehensible customs was that at certain intervals the tribe divided itself into two factitious divisions, each headed by various chiefs, and gambled furiously for many days, one party against the other. They were pugnacious, and in their uncivilised way fought frequent wars. They were remarkably loyal to each other, and treacherous to the foe; brave, and very stoical. "Monogamy was very prevalent." It is remarked that husbands and wives were very fond of each other, and the great body of scientific opinion favours the theory that mothers were much attached to their children. Most tribes were very healthy, and some fine-looking. Such were the remarkable people who hunted, fought, feasted, and lived here until the light came, and all was changed. Other qualities they had even more remarkable to a European, such as utter honesty, and complete devotion to the truth among themselves. Civilisation, disease, alcohol, and vice have reduced them to a few scattered communities and some stragglers, and a legend, the admiration of boyhood. Boys they were, pugnacious, hunters, loyal, and cruel, older than the merrier children of the South Seas, younger and simpler than the weedy, furtive, acquisitive youth who may figure our age and type. "We must be a Morally Higher race than the Indians," said an earnest

American businessman to me in Saskatoon, "because we have Survived them. The Great Darwin has proved it." I visited, later, a community of our Moral Inferiors, an Indian "reservation" under the shade of the Rockies. The Government has put aside various tracts of land where the Indians may conduct their lives in something of their old way, and stationed in each an agent to protect their interests. For every white man, as an agent told me, "thinks an Indian legitimate prey for all forms of cheating and robbery".

The reservations are the better in proportion as they are further from the towns and cities. The one I saw was peopled by a few hundred Stonies, one of the finest and most untouched of the tribes. Of these Laughing Earth had made one, but alas! a few years before she had become

> a portion of the mirthfulness
> That once she made more mirthful.

The Indians occupy themselves with a little farming and hunting, and with expeditions, and live in two or three small scattered villages of huts and tents. But the centre of the community is the little white-washed house where the agent has his office. Here we sat, he and I, and talked, behind the counter. The agent is father, mother, clergyman, tutor, physician, solicitor, and banker to the Indians. They wandered in and out of the place with their various requests. The most part of them could not talk English, but there was generally some young Indian to interpret. An old chief entered. His grey hair curled down to his broad shoulders. He had a noble forehead, brown, steady eyes, a thin, humorous mouth. His cow had been run over by the C.P.R. What was to be done? and how much would he get? The affair was discussed through an interpreter, a Canadianised young Indian in trousers, who spat. Some of the men, especially the older ones, have wonderful dignity and beauty of face and body. Their physique is superb; their fea-

tures shaped and lined by weather and experience into a
Roman nobility that demands respect. Several such
passed through. Then came an old woman, wizened and
loquacious, bent double by the sack of her weekly provision of meat and flour. She required oil, was given it,
secreted it in some cranny of the many-coloured bundle
that she was, and staggered creakily off again.

The office emptied for a while. Then drifted in a
younger man, tall, with that brown, dog-like expression
of simplicity many Indians wear. He was covered by a
large grey-coloured blanket, over his other clothes. He
puffed at a pipe and stared out of the window. The
agent and I continued talking. You must never hurry an
Indian. Presently he gave a little grunt. The agent said,
"Well, John?" John went on smoking. Five minutes later,
in the middle of our conversation, John said suddenly,
"Salt." He was staring inexpressively at the ceiling.
"Why, John," said the agent, "I gave you enough salts
on Thursday to last you a week." John directed his gaze
on us, and smoked dumbly. "Still the stomach?"
inquired the agent, genially. John's expression became
gradually grimmer, and he moved one hand slowly
across till it rested on his stomach. An impassive, signifi-
cant hand. After a courteous pause the agent rose,
poured some Epsom salts out of a large jar, wrapped
them in paper, and handed them over. John secreted
them dispassionately in some pouch among the skins
and blankets that wrapped him in. We went back to our
conversation. Five minutes after he grunted, suddenly.
Again five minutes, and he departed. His wife—a
plump, patient young woman—and his solemn-eyed, fat,
ridiculous son of four, were sitting stolidly on the grass
outside. It obviously made no difference if he took one
hour or seven over his business. They mounted their tiny
ponies and trotted briskly off.

I suppose one is apt to be sentimental about these
good people. They're really so picturesque; they trail
clouds of Fenimore Cooper; and they seem, for all their

unfitness, reposefully more in touch with permanent
things than the America that has succeeded them. And it
is interesting to watch our pathetic efforts to prevent or
disarm the effects of ourselves. What will happen? Shall
we preserve these few bands of them, untouched, to
succeed us, ultimately, when the grasp of our "civilisation" weakens, and our transient anarchy in these wilder
lands recedes once more before the older anarchy of
Nature? Or will they be entirely swallowed by that ugliness of shops and trousers with which we enchain the
earth, and become a memory and less than a memory?
They are that already. The Indians have passed. They
left no arts, no tradition, no buildings or roads or laws;
only a story or two, and a few names, strange and
beautiful. The ghosts of the old chiefs must surely chuck-
le when they note that the name by which Canada has
called her capital and the centre of her political life,
Ottawa, is an Indian name which signifies "buying and
selling". And the wanderer in this land will always be
remarking an unexplained fragrance about the place-
names, as from some flower which has withered, and
which he does not know.

THE ROCKIES

A T Calgary, if you can spare a minute from more important matters, slip beyond the hurrying white city, climb the golf links, and gaze west. A low bank of dark clouds disturbs you by the fixity of its outline. It is the Rockies, seventy miles away. On a good day, it is said, they are visible twice as far, so clear and serene is this air. Five hundred miles west is the coast of British Columbia, a region with a different climate, different country, and different problems. It is cut off from the prairies by vast tracts of wild country and uninhabitable ranges. For nearly two hundred miles the train pants through the homeless grandeur of the Rockies and the Selkirks. Four or five hotels, a few huts or tents, and a rare mining-camp—that is all the habitation in many thousands of square miles. Little even of that is visible from the train. That is one of the chief differences between the effect of the Rockies and that of the Alps. There, you are always in sight of a civilisation which has nestled for ages at the feet of those high places. They stand, enrobed with worship, and grander by contrast with the lives of men. These unmemoried heights are inhuman—or rather, irrelevant to humanity. No recorded Hannibal has struggled across them; their shadow lies on no remembered literature. They acknowledge claims neither of the soul nor of the body of man. He is a stranger, neither Nature's enemy nor her child. She is there alone, scarcely a unity in the heaped confusion of these crags, almost without grandeur among the chaos of earth.

Yet this horrid and solitary wildness is but one aspect. There is beauty here, at length, for the first time in Canada, the real beauty that is always too sudden for mortal eyes, and brings pain with its comfort. The Rockies have a remoter, yet a kindlier, beauty than the Alps. Their rock is of a browner colour, and such rugged peaks and crowns as do not attain snow continually suggest gigantic castellations, or the ramparts of Titans. Eastward, the foothills are few and low, and the mountains stand superbly. The heart lifts to see them. They guard the sunset. Into this rocky wilderness you plunge, and toil through it hour by hour, viewing it from the rear of the Observation-Car. The Observation-Car is a great invention of the new world. At the end of the train is a compartment with large windows, and a little platform behind it, roofed over, but exposed otherwise to the air. On this platform are sixteen little perches, for which you fight with Americans. Victorious, you crouch on one, and watch the ever-receding panorama behind the train. It is an admirable way of viewing scenery. But a day of being perpetually drawn backwards at a great pace through some of the grandest mountains in the world has a queer effect. Like life, it leaves you with a dizzy irritation. For, as in life, you never see the glories till they are past, and then they vanish with incredible rapidity. And if you crane to see the dwindling further peaks, you miss the new splendours.

The day I went through most of the Rockies was, by some standards, a bad one for the view. Rain scudded by in forlorn, grey showers, and the upper parts of the mountains were wrapped in cloud, which was but rarely blown aside to reveal the heights. Sublimity, therefore,

was left to the imagination; but desolation was most
vividly present. In no weather could the impression of
loneliness be stronger. The pines drooped and sobbed.
Cascades, born somewhere in the dun firmament above,
dropped down the mountain sides in ever-growing white
threads. The rivers roared and plunged with aimless
passion down the ravines. Stray little clouds, left behind
when the wrack lifted a little, ran bleating up and down
the forlorn hill-sides. More often, the clouds trailed
along the valleys, a long procession of shrouded, melancholy figures, seeming to pause, as with an indetermi-
nate, tragic, vain gesture, before passing out of sight up
some ravine.

Yet desolation is not the final impression that will
remain of the Rockies and the Selkirks. I was advised by
various people to "stop off" at Banff and at Lake
Louise, in the Rockies. I did so. They are supposed to
be equally the beauty-spots of the mountains. How per-
plexing it is that advisors are always so kindly and
willing to help, and always so undiscriminating. It is
equally disastrous to be a sceptic and to be credulous.
Banff is an ordinary little tourist-resort in mountainous
country, with hills and a stream and snow-peaks beyond.
Beautiful enough, and invigorating. But Lake Louise—
Lake Louise is of another world. Imagine a little round
lake six thousand feet up, a mile across, closed in by
great cliffs of brown rock, round the shoulders of which
are thrown mantles of close dark pine. At one end the
lake is fed by a vast glacier, and its milky tumbling
stream; and the glacier climbs to snowfields of one of
the highest and loveliest peaks in the Rockies, which
keeps perpetual guard over the scene. To this place you
go up three or four miles from the railway. There is the
hotel at one end of the lake, facing the glacier; else no
sign of humanity. From the windows you may watch the
water and the peaks all day, and never see the same
view twice. In the lake, ever-changing, is Beauty herself,

as nearly visible to mortal eyes as she may ever be. The water, beyond the flowers, is green, always a different green. Sometimes it is tranquil, glassy, shot with blue, of a peacock tint. Then a little wind awakes in the distance, and ruffles the surface, yard by yard, covering it with a myriad tiny wrinkles, till half the lake is milky emerald, while the rest still sleeps. And, at length, the whole is astir, and the sun catches it, and Lake Louise is a web of laughter, the opal distillation of all the buds of all the spring. On either side go up the dark processional pines, mounting to the sacred peaks, devout, kneeling, motionless, in an ecstasy of homely adoration, like the donors and their families in a Flemish picture. Among these you may wander for hours by little rambling paths, over white and red and golden flowers, and, continually, you spy little lakes, hidden away, each a shy, soft jewel of a new strange tint of green or blue, mutable and lovely. And beyond all is the glacier and the vast fields and peaks of eternal snow.

If you watch the great white cliff, from the foot of which the glacier flows—seven miles away, but it seems two—you will sometimes see a little puff of silvery smoke go up, thin, and vanish. A few seconds later comes the roar of terrific, distant thunder. The mountains tower and smile unregarding in the sun. It was an avalanche. And if you climb any of the ridges or peaks around, there are discovered other valleys and heights and ranges, wild and desert, stretching endlessly away. As day draws to an end the shadows on the snow turn bluer, the crying of innumerable waters hushes, and the immense, bare ramparts of westward-facing rock that guard the great valley win a rich, golden-brown radiance. Long after the sun has set they seem to give forth the splendour of the day, and the tranquillity of their centuries, in undiminished fulness. They have that otherworldly serenity which a perfect old age possesses. And as with a perfect old age, so here, the colour and the light ebb so gradually out of things that you could swear nothing of the radiance and glory gone up to the very moment before the dark.

It was on such a height, and at some such hour as this, that I sat and considered the nature of the country in this continent. There was perceptible, even here, though less urgent than elsewhere, the strangeness I had noticed in woods by the St. Lawrence, and on the banks of the Delaware (where are red-haired girls who sing at dawn), and in British Columbia, and afterwards among the brown hills and colossal trees of California, but especially by that lonely golden beach in Manitoba, where the high-stepping little brown deer run down to drink, and the wild geese through the evening go flying and crying. It is an empty land. To love the country here—mountains are worshipped, not loved—is like embracing a wraith. A European can find nothing to satisfy the hunger of his heart. The air is too thin to breathe. He requires haunted woods, and the friendly presence of ghosts. The immaterial soil of England is heavy and fertile with the decaying stuff of past seasons and generations. Here is the floor of a new wood, yet uncumbered by one year's autumn fall. We Europeans find the Orient stale and too luxuriantly fetid by reason of the multitude of bygone lives and thoughts, oppressive with the crowded presence of the dead, both men and gods. So, I imagine, a Canadian would feel our woods and fields heavy with the past and the invisible, and suffer claustrophobia in an English countryside beneath the dreadful pressure of immortals. For his own forests and wild places are windswept and empty. That is their charm, and their terror. You may lie awake all night and never feel the passing of evil presences, nor hear printless feet; neither do you lapse into slumber with the comfortable consciousness of those friendly watchers who sit invisibly by a lonely sleeper under an English sky. Even an Irishman would not see a row of little men with green caps lepping along beneath the fire-weed and the golden daisies; nor have the subtler fairies of England found these wilds. It has never paid a steamship or railway company to arrange for their emigration.

In the bush of certain islands of the South Seas you may hear a crashing on windless noons, and, looking up, see a corpse swinging along head downwards at a great speed from tree to tree, holding by its toes, grimacing, dripping with decay. Americans, so active in this life, rest quiet afterwards. And though every stone of Wall Street have its separate Lar, their kind have not gone out beyond city-lots. The maple and the birch conceal no dryads, and Pan has never been heard amongst these reed-beds. Look as long as you like upon a cataract of the New World, you shall not see a white arm in the foam. A godless place. And the dead do not return. That is why there is nothing lurking in the heart of the shadows, and no human mystery in the colours, and neither the same joy nor the kind of peace in dawn and sunset that older lands know. It is, indeed, a new world. How far away seem those grassy, moonlit places in England that have been Roman camps or roads, where there is always serenity, and the spirit of a purpose at rest, and the sunlight flashes upon more than flint! Here one is perpetually a first-comer. The land is virginal, the wind cleaner than elsewhere, and every lake new-born, and each day is the first day. The flowers are less conscious than English flowers, the breezes have nothing to remember, and everything to promise. There walk, as yet, no ghosts of lovers in Canadian lanes. This is the essence of the grey freshness and brisk melancholy of this land. And for all the charm of those qualities, it is also the secret of a European's discontent. For it is possible, at a pinch, to do without gods. But one misses the dead.

1. Stoney Indian camp on Cascade River, Alberta c. 1902.

Public Archives of Canada.

*The reservations are the better in proportion as they are further
from the towns and cities. The one I saw was peopled by a few
hundred Stonies, one of the finest and most untouched
of the tribes.*

From "The Indians".

2. Stoney Indian boys, n.d. *Public Archives of Canada.*

*I suppose one is apt to be sentimental about these good people.
They're really so picturesque; they trail clouds of Fenimore
Cooper; and they seem, for all their unfitness, reposefully more
in touch with permanent things than the America that has
succeeded them.*

From "The Indians".

3. Warriors at the "Stampede", Winnipeg, Manitoba, 1913.
Public Archives of Canada.

4. Indian women and children, Winnipeg, Manitoba, 1913.
Archives of Ontario.

5. Indian horse race, Hazelton, British Columbia, c. 1912.
Public Archives of Canada.

6. The railway station, Laggan, Alberta, 1914. (After 1914 Laggan
was known as Lake Louise.) *Public Archives of Canada.*

7. Chateau Lake Louise, c. 1913. *Public Archives of Canada.*

At one end the lake is fed by a vast glacier, and its milky tumbling stream; and the glacier climbs to snowfields of one of the highest and loveliest peaks in the Rockies, which keeps perpetual guard over the scene. To this place you go up three or four miles from the railway. There is the hotel at one end of the lake, facing the glacier; else no sign of humanity.

From "The Rockies".

V

"YOU think B.C. means before Christ. But it doesn't," Brooke wrote to Sybil Pye from Victoria on 12 September. He had been in the province little more than a week, and had spent most of that time in Vancouver. A pile of mail had awaited him there and he admitted in a letter to Eddie Marsh that he was feeling guilty about not doing enough writing:

> As for my poems. I know I've only sent three. . . . But damn it, what's the good of a friend if he can't sit down & write off a few poems for one at a pinch? That's what I count on your doing, if the editors press. . . . I've a lot half way through, to be finished when I have leisure. I *ought* to have done them in the Rockies. But I had an Episode with a Widow, instead.

His mother had written that she liked his "W. G. articles". He replied that "they're not always very well written" but he thought them "the sort of stuff that ought to interest an intelligent W. G. reader more than the ordinary travel stuff one sees".

It was now commonplace for him to be interviewed in the local papers. As he had noted to Eddie Marsh, many western papers simply reprinted the laudatory article written by Hathaway for the Toronto *Globe*—prefacing it with his poem "Dust". That was the case, for example, in the *Edmonton Daily Bulletin* where he appeared in a column headed "In the

Realm of Women By Penelope". The column itself was dominated by a portrait of Vita Sackville-West whose engagement
to Harold Nicholson had just been announced "after a very
romantic and sensational courtship". "Miss Sackville West,"
the paper explained, was "the daughter of Lady Sackville,
whose right to three million dollars of a legacy was recently
decided by the courts. During the trial the daughter said she
would never marry till her mother's suit was won." The
society pages of the entire English-speaking world had featured the story for months.

Frequently Brooke's poetry was ignored and he was viewed
by the Canadian press as a political journalist. In the *Calgary
News-Telegram* he was called a "special writer" touring Canada "with a view to getting into closer touch with the political
situation". His opinions were predictable. On the naval question: "The Canadian navy should be part and parcel of the
fleet of the British Empire," and on Canada's crippled economy: "I notice that there is a marked tightness in the money
market." That was hardly brilliant, even though most Canadians couldn't believe the boom years had ended and preferred
the euphemism "financial stringency" to the more accurate
word, depression.

By the time Brooke got to the west coast he was considered
by the press to be investigating the "Oriental question". The
Victoria Daily Times reported his opinion that

> the position of British Columbia on the Oriental question is
> little understood in Eastern Canada or in the Old Country...
> and...the impression is generally that the feeling against the
> celestials here is no longer economic but racial and as such is
> not looked on with approval.

He wrote to D. C. Scott in Ottawa, warning him not to
believe everything he read in the papers:

> Out West I have sloughed the poet, and become the Political
> Thinker. Why, I don't know. The papers all interview me on
> The European situation and the Navy Question; and print
> columns and columns of what I never did and never could say.
> So if, out East, you hear me reported as saying 'Old Laurier's
> some guy' or any such thing, you'll know it's a libel.

Brooke wrote to his mother about Vancouver:

> I had several introductions in Vancouver, and only four days.
> It's a queer place, rather different from the rest of Canada.
> More oriental. The country and harbour are rather beautiful
> with great violet mountains all round, snow-peaks in the dis-
> tance. They interviewed me and put (as usual) a quite inaccur-
> ate report of it in the paper, saying I'd come here to investigate
> the Japanese question. In consequence about five people rang
> me up every morning at 8 o'clock (British Columbians get up
> an hour earlier than I) to say they wanted to wait on me and
> give me their views. Out here they always have telephones in
> the bedrooms. One old sea captain came miles to tell me that
> the Japanese—and every other—trouble was due to the fact that
> British Columbia had neglected the teaching of the Gospels on
> the land question. He wasn't so far out in some respects. For
> Canadian politicians & politics are in a most ghastly corrupt &
> rotten state. B. Columbia returns 39 Conservatives and 2
> Socialists to a local house of 41 members. The Conservative
> majority was got by turning the population of every doubtful
> constituency out to build roads for high wages at the public
> expense for six months before the elections. McBride, who's
> now in England, the premier of B.C., had practically no money
> when he entered politics a few years ago; and now he is a
> millionaire. People have done the same all over Canada.

Rupert was right both about British Columbian politics
and Sir Richard McBride, who in 1913 had celebrated ten
years in office. But times were changing. British Columbia's
fragile mining and timber economy had been badly shaken in
the autumn of 1912 when British investments were largely
withdrawn because of European war scares. McBride himself
had gone to England to drum up investment in the province.
And the Oriental question had flared anew shortly before
Brooke's visit. In August of 1913 Chinese and Japanese
strike-breakers had been brought in to the coal mines near
Nanaimo. An enraged mob of white labourers seized the
town, looting and burning, until more than a thousand
troops, special police, and militia moved in to restore order.
Brooke wrote his mother about the Orientals:

> Vancouver is full of Chinese and Japanese and Hindus. The
> Hindus wear their turbans. There is a lot of feeling against all

the Orientals. They come in and underbid the white labour, and get rich and buy land. Some trades they've taken over altogether. When British Columbia, California, and Australia get working together against Japan, there'll be trouble out here. They have anti-yellow riots occasionally.

In Vancouver as well, he spent some time with the Canadian novelist Isabel Ecclestone Mackay. A year before she had published *The House of Windows*, a sensitive story which looked at the plight of the working classes in Canada—particularly the effects of low wages and poor working conditions on women. It had been well received in both the London *Times* and the *Athenaeum*. Mrs. Mackay was also a prolific (if dull) poet so she and Brooke found plenty to talk about.

But Brooke was tiring of Canada—"a most horribly individualistic place, with no one thinking of anything except the amount of money they can make, by any means, in the shortest time". He spent a few days in Victoria and travelled on Vancouver Island. There, he was distressed to read in the papers that Edmund Morris, the painter he had met in Toronto, had drowned in Portneuf in Quebec. It was a sombre note and under its spell he left the country, taking the boat from Victoria on 13 September to Seattle before pushing on south to San Francisco.

Canada, frankly, had left him with mixed feelings. "I'm glad in a way," he wrote to Russell Loines, an American lawyer whom he had visited in New York, "to be out of Canada." He went on:

Theoretically, I hold that Life is more important than Art, that intellectual snobbery is the worst kind, etc. etc. But in practice I do like occasionally seeing people who have heard of, say, Shakespere before, even though we don't discuss it. And the U.S., even where they're ghastly vulgar (as often), are apt to show some—not very healthy—vitality & liveliness. The Canadian is *sehr steif*, as my German friends say of me. Well, I guess the *Westminster* has started printing my insults now: & you'll never speak to me again.... Don't take anything personally. I may have quoted your remarks. I forget. But I probably put them in other people's mouths. It's all a composition.

Brooke's articles in the *Westminster Gazette* ceased with the instalment on the Rockies. He had planned more but there was some confusion as to the number the paper wanted. There was another reason, however, for Brooke's stopping with the Rockies. Somewhere on his trip through British Columbia he lost his notebook. He wrote to the Marchesa Capponi that it "contained 2 months' notes on my travels and unfinished sonnets, and all sorts of wealth . . . *yessir*, isn't it *too* bloody. I've been prostrated with grief ever since. And God knows how I shall get through my articles on Canada."

Included in the Brooke Archive at King's College, Cambridge are two hitherto unpublished fragments entitled "Vancouver" and "Victoria". They appear to have been the beginnings of some further articles and doubtless were prepared by Brooke from memory after he had left the country. They are important not simply because they help to trace Brooke's Canadian journey right across the country, but because, particularly in the one on Victoria, he attempts, as he did with "The Rockies", to come to grips with the country. It is possible that the "Victoria" piece became a working draft for his reflections in "The Rockies". In any case, both drafts end suddenly at a pregnant point.

VANCOUVER

THE train swung and jolted on lower and lower, by foaming rivers, down canons [canyons], past interminable dripping forests. At length the flat; and then we found ourselves running through the rain by a little inlet of dirty brown water, salt in appearance. Four tired Americans and myself stared at each other with a wild surmise. It was a new ocean.

These peoples live very publicly. It is terrifying to a shy man with the secretive instincts of the English, to introduce himself into a Canadian or American hotel. You approach, with the rest of the new comers, an immense counter, shining and public, behind which gleaming, lithe, efficient young men, infinitely genial, infinitely unsympathetic, control and disperse, along the proper channels, to the moment's Destination, baggage, and money, and letters, and you, and checks, and information and the keys of rooms. All around are leather seats and couches, packed with spectators, smoking and spitting. Attendants marshal you into a *queue*. When your turn comes you sign your name in a great volume, and leaning over the counter, whisper without moving your lips, "*What are your charges?*" as if the question had just struck you. Utterly alien to the spirit of the Dialogue, he cries, "ROOM AN' BATH THREE FIFTY UP.

ROOM ALONE TWO DOLLARS UP." There is no chance
for parleying. The multitudes behind are raging with
impatience. A great silence falls on the assembly. Every
one cranes his neck to hear. . . .

VICTORIA

THAT afternoon I had gone fifty miles out of Victoria, up Vancouver Island. When I got back to Victoria it was early evening. I went out and sat on some rocks by the edge of the city, my mind full of the tragic joke that a young man from Western Canada should think China uncivilized. At my feet the smooth Pacific swayed and murmured. I looked westward and southward over forty miles of still evening sea to the American shore and a great range of mountains. The world was silver and pale gold. Across the whole line of these hills, half-way up, was drawn a thin violet line of mist, very straight, and from thence down their skirts hung borders of a mysterious pearly haze. But the summits, the peaks and mighty shoulders, capped and lined with year-long snow, stood clear and desirable against the delicate remote afterwash of sunset. There were no clouds. The water seemed to lie at rest, cleared by the perpetual showers of light that had been falling through it all day, and had washed it from turbulence as rain washes the air. Far down in its darkening green, stones and weeds and points of light were visible. A few gigantic stalks of glossy brown seaweed seemed to be shouldering their slow way shoreward through the calm. The opal light caught them, and passed, and breathed over the waters. There was great peace and beauty in the mountains and the sea.

In a little beach of sand to my left children were playing; they were dressed in white, leaping on and off a half-beached log, laughing, irradiate with the quiet sunset. And a small girl of seven or eight was rollerskating up and down the empty street behind, her thin body curving and bending in her flight. I watched the children and the mountains and thought of Canada. I thought of her possibilities, and of her wealth and corruption and individualism and ugliness. I thought of all the people I had met and talked with, their simplicity and friendliness, the lack of charm of many, the loneliness of some, the dullness and absence of ideal in the young, the strength and beauty of heart and queer purity of mind in certain men and women I had come to know. I wondered what was to be the future of the land. And of all that I had experienced there, I found one scene remaining most vividly and significantly in my mind. It was a group on a little verandah in Winnipeg, in summer after dinner. The air was hot; the wide street, bordered by truly expensive houses, was filled with the motor-cars which every clerk or rather poor man burns to own as soon as he can afford it, or sooner; and one could feel that out west, over the prairie, a black thunderstorm was coming up. There was an Englishman who had been some years in Canada, and a few Canadians— a politician, a lawyer, and an old clergyman. This last was an ardent lover of his country. He had spent his life in social and religious work for her. He could not bear it if any of the rest of us found undue fault with some feature of Canada. But he himself was almost hopeless. By temperament and by profession he was inclined to use other standards in judgement than those of wealth, numbers, or extent of territory. Lack of enterprise in anything except money-making, the absence of a spirit or tradition of public service, the corruption of politics, and the power of the big corporations, all these were his

constant themes. He thought of Canada as of a country
sick almost to death, infected by the neighbourhood of
the United States, diseased with the Financialism which
is the spirit of the age. To "make good" is the motto,
and that means, to make money. Such things, we said,
were true of most of the world. But Canada, he would
have it, was in worse case than other lands. For England
still has some tradition of public service to temper
greed; and though America is a plutocratic state, the
plutocracy is never safe; for all Americans are rebels at
heart. But Canadians mix the docility of the British with
the individualism of the Americans. Nor would he allow
our trite plea that "Canada is a new country". He said
that the East had been growing for two or three
hundred years, and that Greek colonies had not taken
that time to bring beauty and nobility into their lives.
He reminded us that Montreal and Quebec had been
cities when Birmingham was a village and San Francisco
a Spanish mission and there was only a handful of
Savages in Chicago and Seattle was less than a dream.
But it was the result, or cause, of this spirit of the
community, the character of the individual, which
chiefly drew his attention. The deterioration in the
hearts and souls of men terrified him. Greed and selfish-
ness and "materialism" were increasing; the claims of
any ideal growing weaker day by day. There was still
good stuff there. Men of the new world still had the
lesser virtues such as cheerfulness and even physical
courage; but they were rapidly starving to death for lack
of the deeper things. This old man, who had spent many
decades in observing and assisting in the history of the
country he loved, and had gone among all classes and
types of men, gave it as the sum of his experience
that. . . .

1. C.P.R. depot, Vancouver, British Columbia, 1911.
Public Archives of Canada.

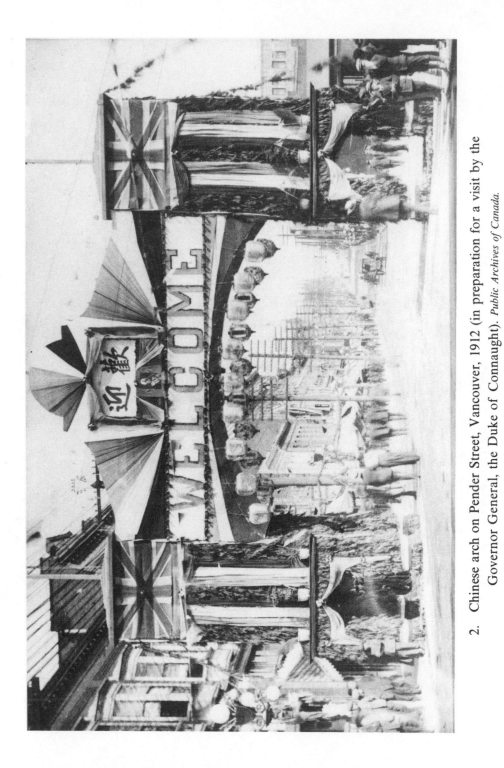

2. Chinese arch on Pender Street, Vancouver, 1912 (in preparation for a visit by the Governor General, the Duke of Connaught). *Public Archives of Canada.*

3. Inner harbour and Empress Hotel, Victoria, British Columbia, c. 1913. *Public Archives of Canada.*

DALLAS HOTEL
ONLY SEA SIDE HOTEL IN VICTORIA B. C.

1547

4. Dallas Hotel, Victoria, B.C., c. 1913. *Brooke Archive, King's College, Cambridge.*

*I'm sitting, wildly surmising, on the edge of the Pacific, gazing
at mountains which are changing colour every two minutes in
the most surprising way. Nature here is half Japanese.*

From a postcard to Sybil Pye, [Victoria], British Columbia,
12 September 1913.

AFTERWORD

RUPERT'S visit to Canada was over; he would not be back even though he had promised Duncan Campbell Scott that he would try to make it to Ottawa by Christmas. The trip had done him good: he had recuperated from his nervous breakdowns of 1912; he had survived apart from his tight circle of Cambridge and London friends; and most important, he was writing again—not just prose for the *Westminster*, but poetry.

He hoped the travel articles wouldn't annoy too many people. Canadians and Americans, he wrote his mother, "are so touchy. But it's absurd to ladle out indiscriminate praise, as most people do." For all his candour Brooke missed the essential truth about both Canada and the United States. Rupert's England, his Cambridge, his London, and his Grantchester were smug middle-class havens, insulated against poverty, unemployment, disease, and squalor. For him these were merely words in a Fabian pamphlet. He moved in a rarefied society: thanks to his friends and contacts he could wrap himself up in it, make it portable, and avoid what a later generation would call "the real world".

Rupert's England was not Wigan Pier, the Salvation Army kettle, the slums of Glasgow, nor London's dockland. If it had been, then perhaps he might have realized that what Canada and the United States had to offer was more valuable than ten thousand soulful Georgian poets. The new world offered hope and opportunity and a chance to make good. That's what was inherent in the lone land, the vast prairies, the ghostless Rockies, the well-tended farmlands of Ontario, and even those ghastly mushrooming cities. And the people who lived here knew it—people from Wigan and Glasgow as well as those "inassimilable lumps" from everywhere else. Canada for them didn't need a past; it had a future.

By the beginning of October Brooke had tired of North America and was looking further afield. He had gone from Vancouver to California which he liked, but as he wrote to his mother from San Francisco, "Canada & America are interesting, but too much like England. I want to see the tropics." It needed only some money borrowed from an American friend to fulfill the wish. On 15 October Brooke stepped off the *S.S. Sierra* at Honolulu and began several months of wandering amongst the Pacific Islands.

From Hawaii he went to Samoa, crossing the Equator en route. There he tramped around, recorded his impressions of the natives, visited Robert Louis Stevenson's grave, and relaxed. He had become restless by the time he reached Fiji. "Oh, it's horribly true what you wrote," he informed Edmund Gosse, "that one only finds in the South Seas what one brings there. Perhaps I could have found Romance if I'd brought it."

Finally, after a "Very English" Christmas in New Zealand, Brooke found his romantic paradise in Tahiti. At once he declared it "the most ideal place in the world". Here he met Taatamata, the native woman who became his mistress, and about whom he wrote some of his best poetry—"Tiare Tahiti", "Retrospect", and "The Great Lover". At last he was at ease in a simple life whose cares centred around eating, sleeping, swimming, wandering, and making love. But after only three months his thoughts turned more and more to England. He had finished his articles for the *Westminster*, he had written some good verse, and he was anxious now to take charge of his life again. Yet travel had become a "habit", and he worried whether his wanderlust would allow him to settle down.

He returned to England, via the United States, where he renewed old friendships and made some new ones. He stopped for several days in Chicago to stay with Maurice Browne of the innovative Chicago Little Theatre and his actress wife, Ellen Von Volkenburg. Chicago surprised Brooke; it was not the intellectual wilderness he expected, but a centre of explosive, creative energy. Carl Sandburg, Ben Hecht, and Charles MacArthur were all part of its excitement. Brooke read his one act tragedy *Lithuania* to the Little Theatre group and Browne determined to produce it. It was eventually staged in Chicago in 1915; critics and audiences alike hated it.

In Washington Brooke saw the Marchesa Capponi, but the spark had gone out of the affair. The attraction probably had been as much Lake Louise as the widow in the first place. From New York, in the company of Maurice Browne and his wife, he took ship for England. He arrived at Plymouth on 6 June 1914. Three weeks later the assassination of Archduke Franz Ferdinand would trigger the First World War.

In the meantime Brooke slid back into his English lifestyle. After his long exile he was delighted with London and the busy social life—largely directed by Eddie Marsh—that engulfed him. And, too, there was Cathleen Nesbitt, still beautiful, still an actress, and more in love with him than ever. It all fell apart in August. Two days before the declaration of war, Brooke asked Eddie Marsh—prophetically—"Do you have a Brussels-before-Waterloo feeling? that we'll all—or some—meet with other eyes in 1915?"

Rupert Brooke went to war as did thousands of other young Englishmen to fight for king and country, national honour, the Empire and to exorcise Kaiscrism. He was also seeking adventure. For Rupert the war engaged both his Victorian idealism and the romantic spirit that had taken him to the South Seas.

By September 1914 he was a Sub-Lieutenant in the Royal Naval Division. Winston Churchill (prompted by Eddie

Marsh) had secured the appointment. By early October, after a few days of scrappy training, Brooke's batallion was in Antwerp, part of the vain British attempt to rescue the Belgians. For the first (and only) time he saw the realities of war in the ragged columns of dazed refugees and the weary faces of defeated soldiers. The experience strengthened his resolve to fight and destroyed the blasé attitude that had allowed him to comment before the actual fighting began: "Well, if Armageddon is *on*, I suppose one should be there." Before Antwerp, afterwards at camp in Dorset, and then on Christmas leave at Rugby, he wrote his most famous poems, the five war sonnets: "Peace", "Safety", the two entitled "The Dead", and "The Soldier".

On 9 February 1915 he sailed with the Royal Naval Division for the Dardanelles, committed to Winston Churchill's futile campaign against the Turks at Gallipoli. There were several stops en route. At Port Said in Egypt Brooke contracted amoebic dysentry; he was not fully recovered when his ship, *The Grantully Castle*, pushed off across the Mediterranean. Two weeks later a tiny abrasion on his lip, perhaps an insect bite, developed into blood poisoning. He had never been robust and was always plagued more than most by colds, influenza, and fevers. Now, his constitution weakened by dysentery, he was easy prey for septicaemia. For a while he seemed to rally and joined a divisional field day on Skyros in the Aegean. That night he was forced to bed and three days later, on 23 April, he died. He was twenty-seven. That same evening he was buried at Skyros in a small olive grove, "one of the loveliest places on this earth", as brother officer Denis Browne wrote home. Browne, a friend from Rugby days, would himself be dead within two months, killed fighting in the trenches at Gallipoli.

One soldier dead in a war that claimed millions—and from a gnat bite at that—is not the stuff of myth. But the atmosphere of 1915 demanded heroes and Brooke with his youth and his beauty and his poetry was a symbol that everyone could grasp. He became the Known Soldier.

The war sonnets were already famous—parts of "The Soldier" had been read from the pulpit of St. Paul's Cathedral. After Rupert's death they became more so. Poetry of any kind rarely catches the public imagination, and patriotic verse too often has a shallow, flag-waving immediacy which loses its meaning once the band stops playing. But Brooke's poetry was a cut above this; it spoke eloquently and passionately of high-born and noble ideals—ideals everyone desperately wanted to embrace in order to give purpose to the war, to account in some fashion for the slaughter of sons, nephews, and the boy next door. Brooke crystallized that feeling. Winston Churchill himself wrote the obituary for *The Times* thus establishing the theme so many others would follow:

> ...The thoughts to which he gave expression in the very few incomparable war sonnets which he has left behind will be shared by many thousands of young men moving resolutely and blithely forward into this, the hardest, the cruellest, and the least-rewarded of all the wars that men have fought. They are a whole history and revelation of Rupert Brooke himself. Joyous, fearless, versatile, deeply instructed, with classic symmetry of mind and body, he was all that one would wish England's noblest sons to be in days when no sacrifice but the most precious is acceptable, and the most precious is that which is most freely proffered.

For weeks thereafter Brooke's name was heard from pulpits, spoken in the streets, and paraded in newspapers and magazines. Byron and Sidney suddenly had company; the poet-soldier myth would remain the dominant impression of Brooke until the end of the war.

After the fighting Brooke was remembered as much for his talent for perpetuating youth as anything else. For the survivors of the war youth and idealism were long lost luxuries. Brooke's poetry reminded them of what they had lost; not all of them liked it. For later generations Brooke was at first quaint and then irrelevant. Now, largely through the bibliographic and archival efforts of Sir Geoffrey Keynes, Brooke's work is considered, if not superb, at least distinguished.

It is tempting to speculate on what Brooke's future might have been had he survived the war. Some of his idealism would surely have been shattered in the ugliness of the trenches, and his poetry—like that of Siegfried Sassoon, Robert Graves, and Wilfred Owen—would have reflected the bitterness, hopelessness, and inescapable misery of the war. His zeal was that of youth; war makes people old in a hurry.

Would he have become a major poet? The question is academic. He may well have turned his hand to the theatre, an interest he mentioned to Duncan Campbell Scott, or to prose, or even as Virginia Woolf suggested, to becoming "Prime Minister, because he had such a gift with people, and such sanity and force". Or, as he feared, he may simply have died in 1950, middle-aged and dispirited, and surrounded by a sobbing family. He didn't have the chance to be great, or a failure, or even ordinary. The war robbed him of the luxury of choice and gave him instead (like Peter Pan in the J. M. Barrie play he loved) eternal youth. It was a poor exchange, one that trapped him forever in the lines of somebody else's poem:

> A young Apollo, golden haired
> Stands dreaming on the verge of strife
> Magnificently unprepared
> For the long littleness of life.

Sherril Schell, Brooke Archive, King's College, Cambridge